Computing
Student Book

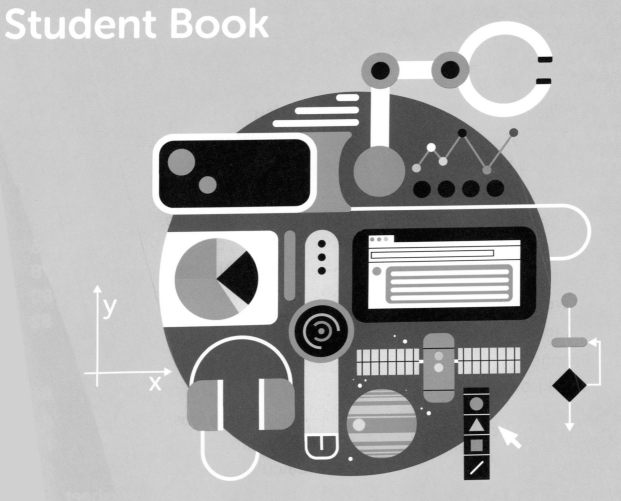

n Page

ard Lincoln

leld

OXFORD

Contents

Introduction   3

1 The nature of technology: Computer networks   4

1.1 What is a network?   6
1.2 Network connections   8
1.3 Network devices   10
1.4 The internet   12
1.5 The changing world of work   14
1.6 Living with the internet   16
Check what you know   18

2 Digital literacy: Searching the world wide web   20

2.1 Searching the web   22
2.2 How search engines work   24
2.3 Search results   26
2.4 Choosing web content   28
2.5 Giving credit   30
2.6 Web challenge   32
Check what you know   34

3 Computational thinking: A test with many questions   36

3.1 Use variables   38
3.2 Ask a random question   40
3.3 Check the answer   42
3.4 Ask 10 questions   44
3.5 Do you want to stop?   46
3.6 Keep trying   48
Check what you know   50

4 Programming: The Hungry Parrot   52

4.1 Set the stage   54
4.2 Control the sprite   56
4.3 Add a second sprite   58
4.4 How do you win the game?   60
4.5 How many flaps?   62
4.6 Chase Your Dinner!   64
Check what you know   66

5 Multimedia: Illustrating a recipe card   68

5.1 Plan a photo shoot   70
5.2 Take digital photos   72
5.3 Share your photos   74
5.4 Improve your photos   76
5.5 Retouch photos   7
5.6 Add photos to a document
Check what you know

6 Numbers and data: My pizza snack bar

6.1 Record your costs
6.2 Calculate your costs
6.3 Calculate your profit
6.4 Create a summary work
6.5 Work independently
6.6 Use your spreadsheet
Check what you know

Glossary

Introduction

Delivering computing to young learners

Oxford International Primary and Lower Secondary Computing is a complete syllabus for computing education for ages 5–14 (Years 1–9). By following the program of learning set out in this series, teachers can feel reassured that their students have access to the computing skills and understanding that they need for their future education.

Find out more at:
www.oxfordprimary.com/computing.

Structure of the book

This book is divided into six chapters, for Year 5 (ages 9–10).

1. **The nature of technology:** Introduction to computer networks
2. **Digital literacy:** Searching for information on the world wide web
3. **Computational thinking:** How we use loops and other structures in programming
4. **Programming:** Using programming skills to control on-screen actions
5. **Multimedia:** Taking digital photographs
6. **Numbers and data:** Using a spreadsheet to help with realistic business activities

What you will find in each unit

- Introduction: An offline activity and a class discussion help students to start thinking about the topic.
- Lessons: Six lessons guide students through activity-based learning.
- Check what you know: A test and activities allow you to measure students' progress.

What you will find in the lessons

Although each lesson is unique, they have common features: learning outcomes for each lesson are set out at the start; learning content delivers skills and develops understanding.

Activity Every lesson involves a learning activity for the students.

Extra challenge Activities to extend students who are able to do more.

Think again Questions check students' understanding of the lesson.

Additional features

You will also find these features throughout the book:

Word cloud The word cloud builds vocabulary by identifying key terms from the unit.

Be creative Suggestions for creative and artistic work.

Explore more Extra tasks that can be taken outside the classroom and into the home.

Digital citizen of the future Advice on using computers responsibly in life.

Glossary Key terms are identified in the text and defined in the glossary at the end.

Assessing student achievement

The final pages in each unit give an opportunity to assess student achievement.

- Developing: This acknowledges the achievement of students who find the content challenging but have made progress.
- Secure: Students have reached the level set out in the programme for their age group. Most should reach this level.
- Extended: This recognises the achievement of students who have developed above-average skills and understanding.

Questions and activities are colour-coded according to achievement level. Self-evaluation advice helps students to check their own progress.

Software to use

We recommend Scratch for writing programs at this age. For other lessons, teachers can use any suitable software, for example: Microsoft Office; Google Drive software; LibreOffice; any web browser.

Source files

 You will see this symbol on some of the pages.

This means that there are extra files you can access to help with the learning activities. For example, Scratch programming files and downloadable images.

To access the files, click 'Download resources' at: **www.oxfordprimary.com/computing**.

Teacher's Guides

For more on these topics, look at the Teacher's Guide that accompanies this book.

1 The nature of technology: Computer networks

You will learn

→ how digital devices can be connected to make networks

→ what the internet is and what services it provides

→ how the internet helps us work together in the modern world

A computer is a powerful tool that we use for working and learning. Connecting computers together makes them more powerful and more useful. When computers are connected, we can use them to communicate with each other. We can share files and search for information on the web. We use networks to connect computers together. In this unit you will learn how networks improve the way we live our lives.

Talk about...

Do you think you will use computers in your job when you leave school? Would you like to work in computing when you leave school? Can you think of any jobs that don't use computers?

Learning outcomes: Explain that digital devices can be connected by communication links; Explain what the internet is and some internet services such as the world wide web; Describe some ways the internet helps us work together in the modern world

Class activity

Here are two statements about how young people should use the internet.

1 "The internet is dangerous. Young people should not be allowed to use the internet."

2 "Young people should be able to use the internet whenever and wherever they choose."

Discuss the statements in your class. List the arguments for and against each statement.

Can your class write your own statement about how young people should use the internet?

network   network device
local area network
wide area network
internet   world wide web
Wi-Fi   server   hub   router

⏻ Digital citizen of the future

Whatever you do in your future life, computers and networks will play an important part. The world of computing changes quickly. You will need to keep your skills up to date so you can use technology at work and at home. At work you will go on training courses to learn new skills. At home you will use the internet to learn new skills. As a good digital citizen, you will help people who have fallen behind with their computing skills.

Did you know?

Today, almost every computer is connected to a network. The biggest network in the world is the internet. The internet has the potential to connect computers wherever they are.

1.1 What is a network?

In this lesson

You will learn:

→ what a computer network is

→ why networks are important at school, at home and in the workplace.

Spiral back

 Last year, you learned about how computers help us learn, work and enjoy our free time. Now you will learn about how computers and other devices are connected and why this is important.

What are networks for?

In offices and schools, computers are usually connected to make a computer **network**.

Networks are complicated to set up. Networks are expensive to run because they need a trained person to fix problems. Most organisations think the cost is worth it because a network has many advantages.

The advantages of networks

- **Communicating:** We can send messages and emails over the network.

- **Sharing:** We use a network to share files and expensive devices like printers.

- **Saving work:** We can save files onto network storage drives. You can use your files on any computer on the network. It is easy to share files with other people.

- **Working together:** Networks help people to work together.

What makes a network?

Four things are needed to make a network:

- **Network devices** to send messages and files between computers, and to store files and applications

- **Cables** to join the devices together

- **Network software** to make the devices work together

- Rules that allow all the parts of a network to work together

You will learn more about network devices and how they are connected in Lessons 1.2 and 1.3.

The two main types of network

- A **local area network** (LAN) joins computers in a single building. A LAN allows people in that building to work together. A school network is a LAN.

- A **wide area network** (WAN) joins computers that are far apart. An organisation with offices in different cities or countries uses a WAN so the employees can work together. The internet is a WAN.

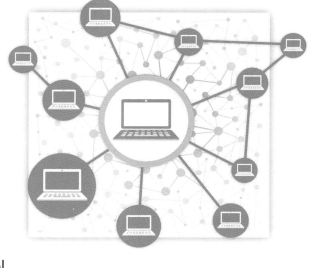

The 'invisible' network

A school network can have 30 or more network devices. It can have 10 kilometres of cable running around the school.

A network is big, but most people don't notice it is there. Most of the equipment is locked away to keep it safe. But there are clues that the network exists. In this unit you will learn to spot the clues.

 Activity

Web Valley Primary School has 60 network connections. The average cable used for each connection is 50 metres long. How many metres of network cable are there in the school? Convert your answer to kilometres.

Extra challenge

Use a spreadsheet to solve the problem in the activity.

Then use your spreadsheet to solve this problem:

Web Valley Secondary School has 140 network connections. The average cable is 65 metres long. How many kilometres of network cable are there in Web Valley Secondary School?

Think again Do you save your school work to the school network? What is your personal area of the school network called? Is there an area on the network that your teacher uses to share files with the class?

Where is the network equipment in your school stored?

In this lesson

You will learn:

→ how computers are connected to a network

→ how to set a strong password and how to keep your password safe.

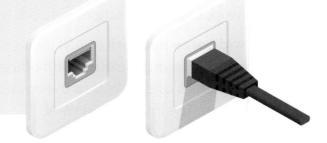

Connecting to a network

There are two ways to connect a computer to a network.

Wired connection

If you use a cable to plug the computer into the network, this is called a **wired connection**. A network cable connects a socket in the computer to an identical socket on the wall of a room.

If you see a socket like the one in the picture, it is a clue that the building you are in has a local area network (LAN).

Wireless (Wi-Fi) connection

You can also connect to a network using a **wireless connection**. This is also called **Wi-Fi**.

Networks use a device called a **wireless access point** (WAP) to provide a wireless connection. If you are close to a WAP, you can connect to a network without using a cable. A place where a wireless connection is available is called a hotspot.

You usually see WAPs high on the wall or on the ceiling.

Laptop and tablet computers usually use a wireless connection to a network. Desktop computers are usually connected to a network with a cable.

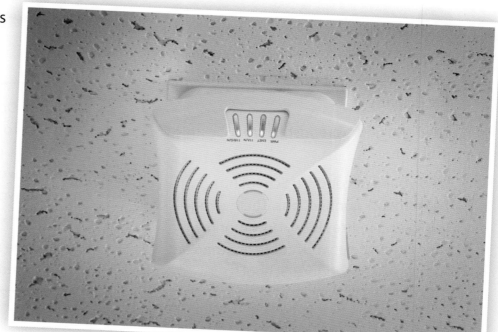

Using a network login

To use a network, you must have a **login**. A login is made up of a user name and a **password**.

Using a login keeps the network safe. Only people who have permission can use the network. Only you can see your own files on the network.

Keep your password safe

You must keep your password safe to protect your information and your work.

- Never tell anyone your password.
- Change your password regularly.
- Choose a strong password.

A strong password

A strong password is difficult for another person to guess. You can use the passphrase method to make a strong password.

1 Think of a short phrase that you can remember. Use two or three short words with eight to twelve characters in total. For example: **'Ginger cats'**

2 Remove the spaces between the words: **Gingercats**

3 Replace some of the letters with other characters that look similar. For example: a → @, e → 3, s → $.

4 This is your new strong password: **Ging3rc@t$**

Activity

Use the passphrase method to make a new strong password for your login.

Extra challenge

Create a poster that reminds students to keep their password safe. Include a guide for creating a strong password. Use your own example of a strong password. Can you suggest different characters to use instead of letters in the phrase?

Explore more

Logins are not just used for school networks. People use logins at work and for online shopping and banking. Ask an adult at home to help you make a list of all the things they use logins for.

Share the passphrase method of creating a strong password with the adult.

In this lesson

You will learn:

→ more about network devices, software and rules.

Devices in a network

A network needs special devices. Each device does an important job in the network.

Servers

A **server** is a powerful computer. A network uses several servers. Each server does a different job.

Print server: When you print a picture or a document, the print server makes sure your file is printed correctly.

File server: This server makes sure your documents are saved correctly.

Email server: This server makes sure your emails reach the right people.

Switches and hubs

Switches are like major junctions in a road traffic system. When you send a message, a switch decides which cable the data needs to travel down to reach the right destination. For example, if you send an email, the switch makes sure your email goes to the email server. A **hub** is a type of switch.

Routers

A **router** connects a network to the internet. Your school network has a router. If you have an internet connection at home, it uses a small router.

How do network devices work together?

The devices in a network work together to get a job done. Here is what happens if you send an email from your school to your home.

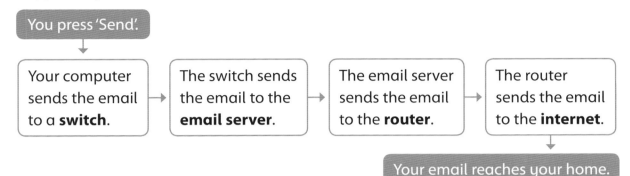

You press 'Send'.

Your computer sends the email to a **switch**. → The switch sends the email to the **email server**. → The email server sends the email to the **router**. → The router sends the email to the **internet**.

Your email reaches your home.

Where are network devices stored?

Network devices are usually stored in a locked room called a **server room**. They are stored in metal cabinets. Sometimes they are stored in small cabinets in classrooms.

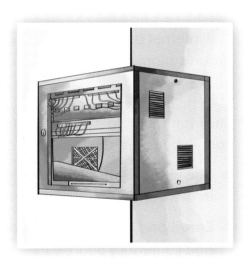

Software and protocols

Two more things are needed to make a network work.

● Software is used to make sure the network runs properly. For example, network software is used to set up user logins.

● All parts of the network must understand each other. The whole network must follow rules so that jobs are done in the correct order. In a network the rules are called **protocols**.

Can you find any clues in your school that tell you the school has a network? If you can, take photos or make drawings as evidence.

 Extra challenge

Read the description of what happens in a network when you send an email. Write a similar description of what happens when you print a document.

 Explore more

If you have an internet connection at home, ask an adult to help you find the router. Be careful not to disturb any cables. Can you see anything that you recognise from studying this unit?

In this lesson

You will learn:

→ what the internet is

→ how the internet is different from the world wide web.

What is the internet?

The **internet** is a wide area network (WAN) that connects computers across the world. It is the biggest network in the world.

People use the internet to communicate and to share things with other people. The internet helps people to learn and work together.

The internet is not owned or controlled by a single person or organisation.

Internet services

The internet is a network of connections. Using those connections, we can make use of a range of services.

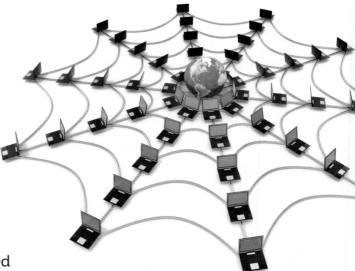

- **The world wide web:** Made of all the web pages in the world.

- **Email and chat:** Ways of sending messages and content to people you know.

- **Video conferencing:** People across the world can meet as if they were in the same room.

- **Streaming:** Games, music and videos can be played on your local device without being downloaded first.

The world wide web

The **world wide web** (www or just 'web') is a part of the internet. The web is all the websites and web pages stored on the internet. You use a web browser to look at web pages on the web. You use a search engine to search for information on the web.

The web is a powerful tool because every web page links to other pages. The links on web pages are called hyperlinks. If you drew lines between the hyperlinks on all the web pages on the web, it would look like a huge spider web.

Computers and the internet

You can use a computer to access all internet services. You use a browser to view the web. You can use other software applications (often called apps) for other internet services such as email.

Many people use a smartphone to access the internet. A smartphone can connect to the internet from anywhere that has a phone signal.

Smart devices

Many home devices are connected to the internet. These are called **smart devices**.

Home security systems can send a warning to your smartphone if sensors detect sound or movement in your home while you are out. You can check security cameras on your smartphone to see if there is an intruder.

You can use your smartphone to control home air conditioning and heating systems so the temperature is comfortable when you get home. You can switch on lights to make it look as if someone is home.

List the main internet services. Say which ones you have used. Give an example.

Extra challenge

Which devices do you use to connect to the internet? Which services do you prefer to access using a smartphone? Which services do you prefer to access using a computer? Give examples.

Research smart home heating or air conditioning systems on the web. List some of the features. How do smart home air conditioning and heating systems help the environment?

In this lesson

You will learn:

→ how computer communication has changed the way people work.

New jobs

The internet has changed the way people work. New jobs have appeared that did not exist before. There are technical jobs like network manager. There are creative jobs like web designer and games programmer.

Old jobs – new skills

The internet has changed existing jobs. A librarian used to work with books that were stored on shelves. Today, the librarian also needs the skills to find information on the web.

Some people have lost their jobs. Automation and robots have replaced low-skilled jobs in factories. Some salespeople in shops have lost their jobs because online shopping has become more popular.

As jobs change, people need to learn new skills. Some people find change exciting. Other people feel threatened by change.

The internet can make it easier to find a new job. There are websites that advertise job vacancies. People can apply for jobs by entering information about their skills on a database. Details of new job vacancies are emailed to them.

Different ways of working

Working in teams

In the past, work teams mostly worked in the same building. The members of a team met regularly face to face to work on projects.

The internet allows people to communicate and share information with colleagues wherever they are in the world. Today, many teams are made up of people working in different cities and even countries. The team members share documents on a network. Many team members never meet face to face.

Teleworking

In the past, people travelled to an office or factory every day to do their work. The internet allows people to communicate using email, internet chat and video conferencing. People can access the information they need to do their work using networks and the internet.

This means that people can work from home. This is called **teleworking**. People don't have to travel so much and can fit work around their home life.

Activity

Describe your dream job when you grow up. How will you use a computer in your job?

Extra challenge

Make an advert for your dream job. Include the computer skills that are needed for the job.

Explore more

Find out what the adults in your family and other grown-up friends think about teleworking. Ask these questions.

1 Do you ever do part of your job from home using an internet link?

2 Could you do more of your job from home using an internet link?

3 Would you like to do more work from home?

Ask any other questions you can think of. Write down the people's answers so you can share them with the class.

In this lesson

You will learn:

→ how the internet affects our lives.

How the internet affects you

The internet has changed the way we lead our lives. Many of the changes have been positive.

Communication: The internet allows you to communicate using text, voice and video. You can share pictures and files. You can use the internet to find advice or to solve a problem.

Information: You use information every day to help you learn, work and lead your daily life. The internet has made information easier and quicker to find.

Convenience: The internet provides 'on-demand' services. This means you can use services when you want them. People use internet banking to pay for things they buy online. You can choose from thousands of shops on the internet. You can download music, games and videos instantly.

Remote control: In Lesson 1.4 you learned about smart devices in the home that allow you to control air conditioning, heating, lighting and security systems remotely.

The dark side of the web

If you use the internet responsibly, you will enjoy its benefits. But be aware that there is a negative side to the internet.

Not everything you read is true

The information on the web is often called content. Some of the content may be false. The writer may make a mistake or they may deliberately write false or misleading content. Some writers may write false content to persuade you to accept their opinions or to sell you something.

Don't trust everyone you meet online

Criminals use the internet. Some criminals use fake emails or websites to try to steal money or personal information. Other criminals trade illegal and counterfeit (fake) goods.

Some people use social media or text messages to send threats or to spread cruel rumours. If someone tries to bully or frighten you online, do not reply to the bully. Report the problem to a responsible adult.

Staying safe on the internet

To stay safe on the internet you need to develop these skills.

> ✓ Technical skills to use the internet safely.
> ✓ Search skills to find what you need, not what others want you to find.
> ✓ Critical skills to judge whether content is reliable.
> ✓ Communication skills to share knowledge.

You will develop some of these skills in Unit 2.

Activity

Imagine that your friend has received threatening text messages from an anonymous person. Write a set of bullet points advising your friend how to deal with the problem.

Extra challenge

Create a poster with the title 'Good internet / Bad internet'. Use one half of the poster to promote the positive side of the internet. Use the other half to warn about the negative side of the internet.

Explore more

Find out how old your parents or grandparents were when the web was invented. Do they remember the first time they used the web?

Check what you know

You have learned

→ how computers and devices can be connected to make networks

→ what the internet is and what services it provides

→ how the internet helps us work together in the modern world.

Test

Think of a device you have used that is connected to the internet. You could choose your smartphone, your computer at school, or another device. Now answer questions about this device.

1 Name the device that is connected to the internet.

2 What is the internet?

3 How is the device connected to the internet – wired or wireless? Explain how you know.

4 When you look at the world wide web on your device, what do you see on the screen?

5 Name one other internet service you could use on the device.

6 Name one piece of equipment that helps your device connect to the internet. What does this equipment do?

7 Who is in charge of the internet?

 **Activity**

Use a word processor to write a report about the internet. Use the headings shown. You can add images to the text if you want.

1 **Internet services:** Describe at least two services offered by the internet.

2 **Working world:** Describe how people might use the internet at work.

3 **Good or bad?** Discuss at least one good and one less good feature of the internet.

Self-evaluation

● I answered test questions 1 and 2.

● I completed section 1 of the activity. I described some positive and negative changes that the internet has caused.

● I answered test questions 1–5.

● I completed sections 1 and 2 of the activity. I described how the internet has changed the way that people work.

● I answered all the test questions.

● I completed all sections of the activity.

Re-read any parts of the unit you feel unsure about. Try the test and activity again – can you do more this time?

2 Digital literacy: Searching the world wide web

You will learn

→ how to find information on the web and describe the sources you use

→ how to choose information you find on the web, and give reasons for your choices

→ how web search engines select and show useful information.

Last year you learned how to use a search engine to find information on the web. Some of the information you find on the web will be correct and reliable. Some of it will be incorrect and misleading. In this unit you will learn how to choose the best information for you.

Talk about...

How do you learn about what is happening in the world? Do you use the web to find news? Can you trust what you read and watch on the web?

Learning outcomes: Obtain information from online sources and describe the sources used; Choose information from online sources, and give reasons for choices; Explain how online searches select and show useful information

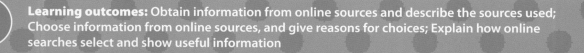

Class activity

What is the most interesting fact that you have learned this week? Your fact can be funny. It can be sad. It can be about a big world event or about something that happened in your town. How did you find out this fact?

Discuss your facts in a small group. Make a list of the facts that your group thinks are the most interesting. Make sure you include one fact from each person in the group.

Do you believe all of the facts are true? Share your findings with the rest of the class.

key word

search engine   bookmark

spider   web crawler   meta tag

the web   web page   website

copyright

The moon is 384,400 kilometres from the Earth.

If you tickle a rat, it laughs!

Did you know?

The world's first **search engine** was invented in 1990 by Alan Emtage. Alan Emtage was born in Barbados but moved to Montreal, Canada, to study at McGill University. His job at the university was to help other students find articles on the internet. He wrote a search engine to save himself time. He called his search engine Archie.

In this lesson

You will learn:

→ four golden rules to help you to search the web.

Spiral back

 Last year you learned how to carry out basic world wide web searches. You learned how to use a search engine to find information quickly on the web. In this lesson you will review the search techniques that you learned last year.

Four golden rules

1 Choose the right key words

Make sure you understand the question you need to answer. Before you enter anything into your search engine:

- Make a list of **key words**.

- Underline the most important key words.

Make sure that the question you type in the search engine contains the important key words. Your question does not need to include punctuation or short joining words like 'is' and 'the'.

2 Choose the right search engine

There are many search engines that you can use. Google, Bing and Yahoo are examples. Try using different search engines. Find out which one works best for you.

Some search engines are designed for young people. The advantages of using a child-friendly search engine are:

- The links are easier for you to read and understand.

- You are less likely to see unsuitable web pages.

- There are fewer adverts.

3 Bookmark your favourite sites

Adding a **web page** to your **bookmarks** makes it easy to find next time you want to use it. You don't have to search for the page again. You click on the link in your bookmarks list and go straight to the page.

Your bookmarks can be a good place to start a search. **Websites** you have found useful in the past might provide the information you need.

4 Try again

Sometimes a search does not give you the information you need. If that happens, try again.

- Try to think of different key words.

- Will a different search engine give better results?

- Will any of your bookmarked pages lead you to helpful information?

Activity

Use a search engine to answer these questions.

1   What is Tungurahua, and where is it?
2   What happened at Tungurahua in March 2016?
3   Find a picture of Tungurahua.
4   Find one interesting fact about Tungurahua.
5   How do you pronounce Tungurahua?

Think again Work in a small group. Discuss websites that you have found useful in your studies. Make a list of the best websites you have found. Why do you like them? What subjects do these websites help with? Present your list to the class.

Extra challenge

Search the web to find the name of this bird.

Hint: To get a list of key words, type the things you see in the picture, such as 'black head'. What else do you see? Do an image search and find a picture that matches this one.

Which combination of key words worked best?

In this lesson

You will learn:

→ how a search engine finds web pages to answer your search questions.

How large is the web?

At the start of 2019 there were 1.9 billion (1,900,000,000) websites on the web. It is easy to imagine what a small number like 10 or 100 looks like. It is more difficult to imagine what a large number like 1 billion looks like.

Think about this book:

● This lesson contains 500 words.

● The complete book contains 25,000 words.

● A pile of 76,000 books would contain 1.9 billion words. That is the same as the number of websites on the web.

● The pile of books would be 400 metres tall.

● That is half the height of the world's tallest building, Burj Khalifa.

How does a search engine work?

When you enter a web search, your question is sent over the internet to a search engine. The search engine uses a powerful computer to look for matches to your key words. A list of links is displayed on your screen.

A search engine would take a very long time to search all 1.9 billion websites on the web. To be able to send you a list of links quickly, the search engine must work in a different way.

Spiders and web crawlers

A search engine uses **web crawling** to search the web. The search engine sends a piece of software called a **spider** to crawl around the web and collect information.

When a spider reaches a web page, it records every word on the page and counts how many times each word is used. Then the spider follows links on the web page and carries out a word count on each new page it finds. Eventually, the spider will visit and record every web page on the web.

Search engine index

The spider software sends the information it collects back to the search engine. The information is stored in a special list called an **index**. When you enter a search question, the search engine searches its index. The index is very large, but searching it is much quicker than searching the whole web.

A search engine compares each key word in your search question to the words stored in its index. It ignores short joining words like 'the', 'what' and 'why'. These words appear on every web page so won't help in a search.

The search engine uses an **algorithm** to compare websites in its index with the key words in your web search. The algorithm chooses the web pages to answer your question.

 **Activity**

Copy this search question: 'What is the longest river in Africa?'

Draw circles around all the words that the search engine will ignore. What is the answer to the question?

 Extra challenge

A search engine uses an algorithm to choose websites to answer a web search question. What is an algorithm? Use the knowledge you have already gained in this course. Search the web for more information if you need to.

 Think again

Carry out a web search to find a video or animation that explains how a search engine works. Watch the video and make notes. Bookmark the video that you find most useful.

Search results

In this lesson

You will learn:

→ how a search engine shows the links it finds.

How many pages?

The web contains 1.9 billion websites. Whatever question you ask, a search engine will find many matching pages.

When a search engine shows a list of links it includes the total number of pages it found. The search shown in this image has found 722,000,000 results.

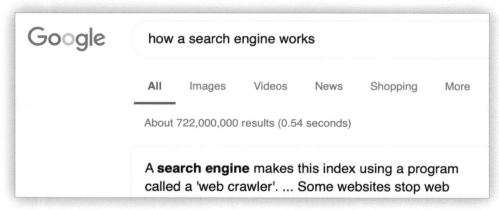

You can make the list shorter by adding more key words to a search. However, you do not usually need to do this.

How a search engine sorts results

A search engine tries to put the most useful links at the top of the list of results. It uses several methods.

- **How popular is a page?** The most popular web pages are shown on the first page of search results. A page is popular if many other sites link to it.

- **How up to date is a page?** Web pages that change often are shown near the top of the search results. Adding new information to a web page is called updating.

- **Can the website be trusted?** Websites that a search engine trusts are shown near the top of the results. This does not mean that you can believe everything you see on websites near the top of the list. You still need to check the facts.

- **Which pages have you looked at before?** A web browser keeps a list of websites you have looked at. The search engine uses this information to predict which websites you will want to see in the future.

Adverts

Most search engines show adverts at the top of the list of results. The owners of these websites pay for the adverts. Adverts are not always relevant to your search.

Trusted site →
Advert →

✓ A brief history of the Galápagos Islands
[Ad] www.journeylatinamerica.co.uk/ ▼
★★★★★ Rating for journeylatinamerica.co.uk: 4.8 - 185
Browse Our Range Of Great Latin America Holidays.
Contact Us · Our Holidays

Meta tags

The owner of a website wants the world to see their pages. One way they can do this is to use **meta tags**. Meta tags are like key words. They are single words that describe a web page.

Web developers add meta tags to the pages they create. People who read a web page cannot see the meta tags, but search engines can see them. If any key words in your search question match the meta tags on a web page, the search engine shows that page near the top of the results list.

 **Activity**

Carry out another web search about Tungurahua. How many results does the search return? Add some more key words to your search. What happens to the number of results?

 Extra challenge

How many adverts are shown when you search for Tungurahua? What are the adverts for? Do the adverts give you any useful information?

 Think again

Carry out a web search for more information about how search engines work. How many adverts are at the top of the list of results? How many of the adverts give you useful and relevant information?

In this lesson

You will learn:

➔ how to choose information carefully from the world wide web.

Can you trust web content?

A web search will provide you with links to many web pages. The links lead to information you can use to complete a project. How will you decide which web pages to use and which to reject?

Sometimes content on web pages is wrong. The person who wrote the content may have made a mistake or the information may be out of date. Sometimes the writer of a web page may deliberately try to mislead you.

Checklist for choosing web content

Ask the questions in this checklist to help you to choose content that is correct, reliable and relevant.

1 **Who wrote the content?**

Who owns the website? Websites that belong to governments, charities, universities or other large organisations are usually reliable sources of information.

Who wrote the web page? It is a good sign if the writer has included their name on the web page. Sometimes web pages also include the writer's job title and contact details.

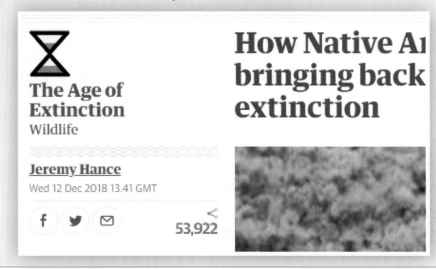

2 Is the content up to date?

Can you find the date when the web page was last updated? Having up-to-date information is important. It is very important in computer studies because technology changes quickly. It can be less important for subjects like history and mathematics.

3 Is the page appropriate for your age?

Content: Can you understand the content or is it too complicated for you? Is there more detail than you need? Is the content too simple for you?

Language: Are there too many words that you don't understand? Are the sentences too long? This is especially important if you are reading content in a second language.

4 Is the content relevant?

Does the page answer your search question? A web search will find many interesting and well-written pages. Which pages provide the information you need?

5 Does the page give you facts or opinions?

Facts: A fact is something that you can check to find out if it is true.

Opinions: An opinion is a what someone thinks or feels.

Does the page give you facts to help you to make up your own mind? Or is the writer giving their opinion to try to persuade you to agree with them?

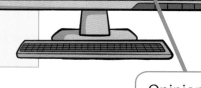

Fact

World internet use

"More than half of the people in the world use the internet."

"People use the internet too much."

Opinion

Activity

Choose a web page you have visited during this unit. Use the checklist in this lesson to write a report about the page.

Explore more

Ask a member of your family to suggest a web page you can both look at. Working together, complete the checklist shown on this page. What does your family member think of the website? Good or bad?

Extra challenge

Search the web for information about the impacts of climate change. Find a page that you like. Is the page mainly facts or opinions? Give one example of each.

In this lesson

You will learn:

→ what copyright is

→ how to give credit to another person's work.

What is copyright?

If you create something, you have **copyright**. Copyright means that you own the work you have created.

Copyright protects the person who created the work. Copyright means that other people:

● cannot copy that work

● must ask for the copyright owner's permission to use or share the work

● must say who created the work.

Using other people's work in your school work

● Make sure you have permission. You can usually use small amounts of other people's work in projects and assignments without asking. If you are not sure, check with your teacher.

● Give credit to the person who created the work.

Giving credit for work you use

If you use part of someone else's work, you must say who created the work. Your credit should include these four pieces of information:

Zheng Ying, Saving the Whales, thedailynews.com, October 2019

- Author
- Title of the article or web page
- Website
- Date the work was created or the date you accessed the website

You may not be able to find all four pieces of information. Use all the information you can find.

Using photos in your work

Photos can make your projects look special. A photo can explain an idea more clearly than words alone.

Some photographers and artists allow people to use their work free of charge. They use a creative commons licence. To find creative commons images, use a web search such as 'creative commons free images tiger'.

Click on the 'Images' tab in your search engine to see photos that you can use. Remember to include a credit.

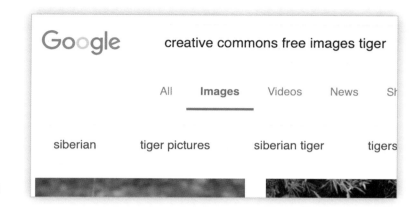

Plagiarism

It is good to use information you have found on the web in your school work. Quotes and facts from experts will improve your work. Pictures will add impact to your projects and assignments.

However, never pretend that another person's work is your own. That is called **plagiarism**. Always credit another person's work. Be confident! You can create great work yourself.

 **Activity**

In Lesson 2.4 you found a web page about the impacts of climate change. Go back to the page and find a piece of text you would like to quote. Copy and paste the quote into a document. Add a credit at the end of the quote.

Extra challenge

Find a creative commons photo that illustrates the quote you used in the activity. Add the photo to your document. Add a credit for the photo.

 Think again

Why does crediting another person's work matter? If it is on the internet, why not just use it? How would you feel if someone copied your work and claimed it was their own?

In this lesson

You will:

→ use the skills and knowledge you have learned in this unit to complete a team web challenge.

The task

Work in a team to create a set of fact sheets. Choose the topic for your fact sheets. Here is an example.

Big cat fact sheets: Each fact sheet will be about one big cat (for example, lion, puma, tiger, cheetah, leopard, jaguar). The fact sheets will all have the same design and the same headings.

Here are some more ideas: famous scientists, football teams, popular singers, capital cities, endangered species.

BIG CATS FACT SHEET: AFRICAN LION

Fun facts

- Lions sleep for 20 hours a day.
- You can hear a lion's roar from 8 km away.
- A lion cannot purr.

Facts	
Home	Southern and eastern Africa
Habitat	Grasslands
Food	A lion eats large animals such as zebra, antelope and wildebeest. Lionesses do most of the hunting.
Families	Lions live in groups called prides. Young lions are called cubs.
Physical features	Male lions have a mane. A male lion weighs 180 kg. A female weighs 150 kg. The lion is the second largest big cat.
Speed	A lion can run at 80 kph over short distances.
Endangered?	Lions are a vulnerable species. Their numbers are declining.

1 Plan your work

Before you start the challenge, plan how your team will work.

- What topic will you choose?

- How will you divide the work between the team members?

- How will you design your fact sheets? What headings will you use? Where will you put photos?

2 Choose websites

Before you start to collect information, each team member should carry out a web search and choose a relevant website. Then decide together which websites you will use to collect information.

3 Collect your facts

Research the information you need. Copy and paste the information into a blank word processor document. You will put it into your fact sheet design later.

4 Create your fact sheets

When you have collected enough information, transfer the information into a fact sheet. Remember to work as a team to make sure your fact sheets all look the same.

Activity

Working in a team, divide up the work you have to do. Create several fact sheets about your chosen topic.

Be creative

Make your fact sheets look interesting and professional. Which fonts and heading sizes will you use. Which colour combinations look best? Try looking at some fact sheets online for design ideas.

Extra challenge

Discuss the web challenge with your team. Was it a success? What websites have been particularly helpful? Were any of the topics too hard or too easy?

Think again

Make a list of the websites you used for this task. Rate how useful each one is.

Check what you know

You have learned

→ how to find information on the web and describe the sources you use

→ how to choose information you find on the web, and give reasons for your choices

→ how web search engines select and show useful information.

Test

Look at the picture and answer the questions.

1 Which words are the important key words in this search question?

   'What is the fastest car in the world?'

2 The picture shows a search engine in a web browser. What is a search engine?

3 Why is it important to check the date of information you find on the web?

4 What does a web crawler do?

5 A search engine uses different methods to make sure relevant websites are near the top of the list of search results. State three of these methods.

 **Activities**

Carry out a web search to find information about the wildlife in China. Look at some of the websites in the search engine's list of results. Choose the website you think is best for you to find out information. Then answer the questions below.

1 List the key words that you used in your web search.

2 Write down two pieces of information about wildlife in China that you found in your search.

3 List three websites you thought were useful.

4 Which website did you choose as the best?

5 Give reasons why you chose the website. Give as much information as you can about the website you chose.

Self-evaluation

● I answered test questions 1 and 2.

● I completed activities 1 and 2. I carried out a web search using key words. I found out some information about wildlife in China.

● I answered test questions 1–4.

● I completed activities 1–4. I carried out a web search and found three useful websites. I chose the best website to find out about wildlife in China.

● I answered all the test questions.

● I completed all the activities.

Re-read any parts of the unit you feel unsure about. Try the test and activity again – can you do more this time?

3 Computational thinking: A test with many questions

You will learn

→ how to plan a program that includes a loop

→ how to use conditional loops and counter loops

→ how to use random numbers in a program.

In this unit you will use the Scratch programming language to write programs.

You will make a test for students to practise times tables. Your test will ask random multiplication questions. The program will tell the user if they get the questions right or wrong.

Your program will use a loop. A **loop** is a program structure. Any commands inside the loop will repeat. You will learn about the different types of loop and how to use them.

Talk about...

In this unit you will make and use **random** values. Random values are unpredictable – you don't know what they are going to be. Many computer games use random values to make the games more interesting and varied.

Think of the computer games you know. Which parts of the game might be random? How do random values make the game more exciting?

Class activity

Write the numbers 1 to 12 on pieces of paper. Put the pieces of paper in a bag. One student takes two numbers from the bag and reads them out. The other students multiply the two numbers together. The first student to say the correct answer is the winner.

Give one point to the winner. Pass the bag to the winner. Now it is their turn to pick two numbers.

For extra challenge, add larger numbers to the bag. That makes the multiplications more difficult.

Learning outcomes: Create and describe an algorithm that includes a loop; Create a program with a loop controlled by an exit condition

Did you know?

Tetris is a computer game. You fit coloured shapes together. There are seven different coloured shapes. Tetris uses a computer program called Random Generator. Random Generator picks a random sequence of seven shapes. There are 5040 possible sequences and they all have the same chance of being picked.

Digital citizen of the future

In this unit you will make a program to help students learn. Computers are used to support education and training. This means you can keep learning all your life, even after you are grown up and leave school.

In this lesson

You will learn:

→ how to plan a program that uses variables and start to make the program.

Spiral back

Last year, you learned how to make and use variables in Scratch programs. If you need help with making variables in this lesson, look back at the lessons in Student Book 4.

The requirement

Before you plan a program, you must decide what the program requirement is. In this unit you will create a program to meet this requirement:

Make a program for a student so they can practise the seven times table.

Program plan

Before a programmer starts work, they make a **program plan**. A program plan sets out the steps to solve a problem. Another word for a plan to solve a problem is an **algorithm**.

A program plan sets out the inputs and outputs of a program. It also sets out the processes done by the computer, such as calculations.

Here is a plan for this program:

Input: Prompt with a question (for example, 'What is 7 times 5?').

Input the user's 'answer'.

Process: Store the 'solution' to the question.

Compare the user's answer to the solution. Do they match?

Output: If the answer matches the solution, output 'You got it right!'

Else, output 'You got it wrong!'

The word 'else' is used in programming. In this example, the computer will output 'You got it wrong!' if the answer does not match the solution.

Variables

A **variable** stores a value. You give every variable a name. Then you can use the value in your program. Two variables are mentioned in the program plan.

In Scratch there is a ready-made variable called 'answer'. You can make a sprite ask a question. The user's answer is stored in 'answer'.

You will also make a new variable called 'solution'. This variable will store the correct solution to the question.

Click on 'Make a Variable'.

Type the variable name 'solution'.

The variable name is ticked. That means it will show on the main screen. Click to remove the tick. You don't want the user to see the solution.

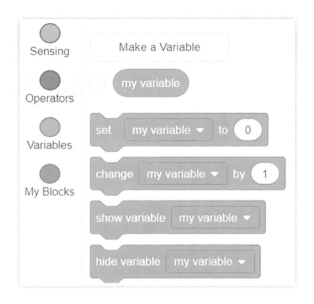

Scratch program

The finished Scratch progam is shown opposite.

This program matches part of the program plan.

- It asks a question.

- It stores a solution.

In the next lesson you will extend the program to match the whole plan.

 Activity

Start Scratch. Create the program shown in this lesson. You can use any 'seven times' question.

Click on the sprite to run the program. The sprite asks a question. There is a box to enter your answer.

Save the program. Open the 'File' menu and select 'Save to your computer'.

Think again
The variables in this program are called 'solution' and 'answer'. Why are these good variable names? Think of alternative variable names which would be just as good.

 Extra challenge

Extend the program to tell the user if their answer is right or wrong.

In this lesson

You will learn:

→ how to plan and create a program that uses a random number.

Make a better plan

The requirement is to create a program that allows the user to practise the seven times table. In the last lesson, you created a program that asks a question. The program always asks the same question.

It will be better if the program asks a different 'seven times' question each time. That will give the user more practice of the seven times table.

In this lesson, you will change the program so that it asks a different 'seven times' question every time you run it. Here is the improved plan.

Input: Make a **random** number.

            Ask "What is 7 times the random number?"

            Input the user's 'answer'.

Process: Calculate the 'solution' to the question.

            Compare the user's answer to the solution. Do they match?

Output: If the answer matches the solution, output 'You got it right!'

            Else, output 'You got it wrong!'

In the last lesson you made a new variable called 'solution'. Now make another variable called 'random'. This variable will store the random number.

Set a random value

This program uses a random value. The computer will pick the random value. The value could be different every time.

Green blocks are 'Operators'. They make new values. This block will pick a random value from 1 to 10. Change the higher value to 12.

Fit these two blocks together to give the random value to the new 'random' variable.

This block goes at the start of the program.

Ask a random question

The 'join' operator joins two values together. When you find this operator on the Scratch website it joins 'apple' and 'banana'. Change the operator so it joins 'What is 7 times' to the 'random' variable.

Now this block makes a random question.

The growing program

Now fit all the blocks together to create the program. Here is the program so far.

- The program makes a random number.

- It asks a random question.

Start Scratch. Create the program shown in this lesson.

Run the program several times. The sprite will ask a random question every time.

Save the file.

Extend your program. Add a second random variable. Name the two random numbers 'random1' and 'random2'. Make a question that asks the user to multiply the two random numbers.

Run the program 10 more times. Keep a tally of the random number that appears each time. Do some numbers appear more often than others?

Because the numbers are random, every number has the same chance of appearing. The tally count for each number should be the same. The more times you run the program, the more even the balance should be. If you have time, run the program lots more times to check this.

In this lesson

You will learn:

→ how to do calculations using random numbers.

Spiral back

If you have never used the 'if… else' block before, review Unit 3 in Student Book 4.

Find the solution to the question

In Lesson 3.1 you wrote a simple program to ask a question. The computer always asked the same question: 'What is 7 times 5?' The solution was 35.

In Lesson 3.2 you made a new program. The question changes each time you run the program. The solution also changes each time.

Now you will change the program so the computer works out the solution to the question. You will use the multiplication operator. It will multiply seven by the random number. The symbol for multiply is *

Make this block.

Store the solution

You know how to make variables. Make a variable called 'solution'.

Use the block shown below to set the variable 'solution' to the calculated value.

Now the variable called 'solution' stores the correct answer to the question. Add the completed block to the program.

Complete the program

Now you can complete the program. Use an 'if… else' block. Compare 'answer' to 'solution', and output 'You got it right!' or 'You got it wrong!'.

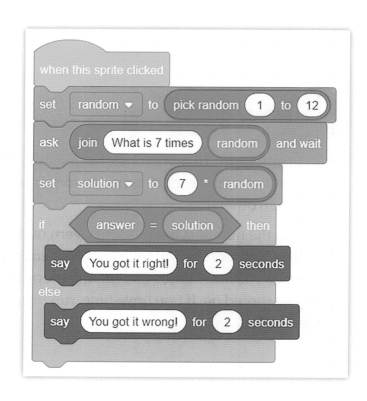

 **Activity**

Load the program you created in the last lesson. Add the extra commands shown in this lesson to complete the program. Run the program to make sure it works. You can run the program many times. The question will usually change each time. But because the question uses a random number, sometimes you will see the same question twice.

 Extra challenge

Put the whole program in a 'forever' loop. The sprite will keep asking random questions until you halt the program.

Hint: To halt the program you click on the red stop sign.

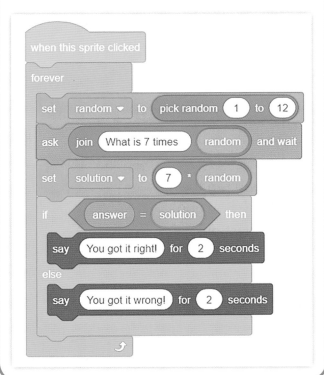

 **Be creative**

Change the sprite and the backdrop to make the test more interesting for students. For example, you could choose a shark in the ocean or a beetle in a forest.

 Think again

What other types of calculation can you do in Scratch? Investigate what other operator blocks are available. How can you use them to make test questions?

3.4 Ask 10 questions

In this lesson

You will learn:

➔ how to plan a program that includes a counter loop.

Spiral back

 Learn about the forever loop in Student Book 4.

Exit condition

If you have used Scratch before, you may have used a 'forever' loop. Any commands inside this loop will be repeated 'forever' (until the program stops).

There are other types of loop that you can use.

The way that the program stops the loop is called an **exit condition**. It is how you 'exit' from the loop.

Types of loop

There are two main types of loop. They have different exit conditions.

- A **counter loop** (or **fixed loop**) repeats a set number of times.
- A **conditional loop** (or **condition-controlled loop**) is controlled by a logical test.

In this lesson you will plan and create a program with a counter loop.

Change the plan

The program you have made asks one question each time you run the program. A more useful test will ask many questions. In this lesson you will extend the program so that the sprite asks 10 random questions.

Here is the new program plan.

Repeat until there have been 10 loops.

Input: Ask a question and get the user's answer.

Process: Calculate the solution to the question.

Output: If 'answer' = 'solution', output 'You got it right!'

             Else, output 'You got it wrong!'

Go back to the top of the loop.

Counter loop

Here is the block that makes a counter loop.

You can see that it counts to 10. Then the loop stops. You could change the value to change the number of times the loop repeats.

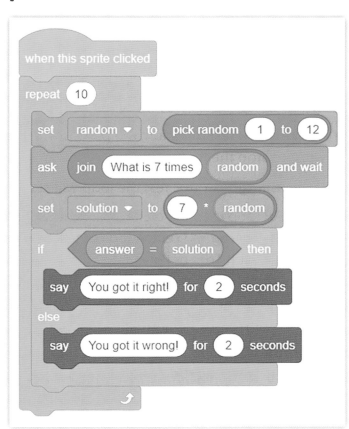

Extend the program to match the plan

All the commands in the program must go inside the counter loop. That is because everything must be repeated each time. The completed program is shown opposite.

Activity

Load the 'seven times table test' program you made in Lessons 3.1 and 3.2. Extend the program so that it uses a counter loop. Run the program to make sure it works. Save the file.

Think again

Make a neat version of the program plan. You could write the plan by hand or use a word processor.

Extra challenge

The program you have made always asks 10 questions. Some people might like a different number of questions.

Before the loop starts, ask the user how many questions they want. Then set the number of repeats to the user's answer.

In this lesson

You will learn:

➔ how to plan and create a program with a conditional loop.

Conditional loop

In the last lesson you created a program with a counter loop. It loops exactly 10 times. The test has exactly 10 questions.

In this lesson you will change the program.

- Before every test question, the program will ask the user if they want to stop the test.
- If the user types Y (for Yes) the loop will stop.

This type of loop is called a conditional loop. A conditional loop is controlled by a **logical test**. A logical test compares two values. It gives the result True or False.

Change the plan

Here is the new program plan.

Repeat until the user types 'Y'.

Input: Ask a question and get the user's answer.

Process: Calculate the solution to the question.

Output: If 'answer' = 'solution', output 'You got it right!'

              Else, output 'You got it wrong!'

Input: **Ask 'Do you want to stop?'**

Go to the top of the loop.

You must put the question 'Do you want to stop?' inside the loop. That gives the user the chance to stop after every question.

Create the test

Your program will ask the user if they want to stop. If the user types 'Y' the program will stop.

This block compares the user answer to the letter Y.

Make this test block.

Conditional loop

Here is the block that makes a conditional loop.

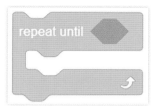

This type of conditional loop is called a **repeat until loop**. It starts with a logical test. The commands inside the loop will repeat until the logical test is True.

● Add the logical test at the top of the loop.

● Add the question 'Do you want to stop?' inside the loop.

The loop will repeat until the answer to the question is Y.

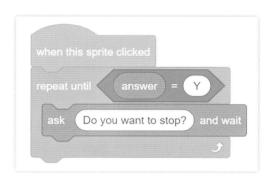

The finished program

All the other commands you have made go inside the loop. These commands will repeat until the logical test is True.

The finished program is shown opposite.

 **Activity**

Create the program shown in this lesson. Run the program to make sure it works. The test should stop if you type 'Y'.

Note: The program will not run again. That is because the computer remembers your last answer 'Y'. You will learn how to fix this problem. But for now, close the program when you have used it one time. Open it again to use it a second time. That will clear the answer.

 Extra challenge

This program will not run two times in a row. That is because the computer remembers the user answer.

Fix this problem by storing the user answer as a variable. For example, it could be called 'stop'. Then set this variable to 'N' before the loop starts.

 Think again Write a short guide to the test you have made. In your guide, explain to other students what happens if they run the program.

In this lesson

You will learn:

→ another way to use the conditional loop

→ the advantages and disadvantages of using a conditional loop.

This is a more challenging lesson. Try this lesson if you have completed all the other activities in this unit. Start a new Scratch program for this lesson.

Make a difficult question

The test you made has simple questions to practise the seven times table. In this lesson you will create a test with just one question. But it will be a difficult question.

Here are some different ways to ask a difficult question.

- Use the 'ask' block to ask one difficult question.

- Use a big random number, up to 50 or even more.

- Ask a different type of maths question, for example division or subtraction.

Work out the solution

Make a variable called 'solution'. You already know how to do this.

Now set the value of the solution. It must be the correct solution to your difficult question. You must work out how to do this.

Here are some examples to help you. You only need to do one.

Use a conditional loop

Now you will add a conditional loop to the program. Every conditional loop is controlled by a logical test. In Scratch the loop will repeat until the test is True.

The loop in this program will ask the user to try again each time they enter a wrong answer. The loop will stop when the user gives the correct answer.

Your program might not look exactly like this. It depends what your difficult question is.

Advantages and disadvantages

Using a conditional loop to get the answer to a question has advantages and disadvantages.

Advantages are benefits or good points. These are some advantages of using a loop to get the answer to a question:

- The user gets lots of chances to answer.

- The user can keep trying until they get the answer right.

Disadvantages are problems or bad points. This is a disadvantage of using a loop to get the answer to a question:

- If the user can't get the right answer, they can't stop the loop. They can't move on to a new question.

 **Activity**

Start Scratch. Create a program that asks a difficult question.

Use a conditional loop to ask the user to try again if they get the answer wrong.

Run the program to make sure it works.

Save the file.

 Extra challenge

Extend the program so the user can choose how big or small the numbers are.

Hint: Think about the block that sets a random number. What happens if you change the larger number in this block?

 Think again

This program asks the user a question until they get it right.

Write down the advantages and disadvantages of this type of program.

Check what you know

You have learned

→ how to plan a program that includes a loop

→ how to use conditional loops and counter loops

→ how to use random numbers in a program.

Test

In this unit you created a program with a counter loop. Think about the work you did.

What is 7 times 3?

1 Think of the program you created. Say in your own words what the program did.

2 Say what actions in your program were repeated inside the counter loop.

3 Make a simple plan for a program you made that includes a counter loop.

4 Explain the difference between a counter loop and a conditional loop.

 **Activities**

In this program the sprite asks a random subtraction question.

1 Create this program. Add a 'forever' loop so the sprite asks lots of questions.

2 Adapt the program so the sprite asks exactly three questions.

3 Adapt the program to use a condition-controlled loop.

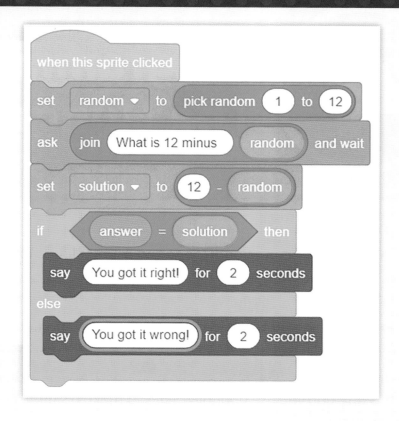

Self-evaluation

- I answered test questions 1 and 2.

- I completed activity 1. I created a program with a 'forever' loop.

- I answered test questions 1–3.

- I completed activities 1 and 2. I created a program with a counter loop.

- I answered all the test questions.

- I completed all the activities.

Re-read any parts of the unit you feel unsure about. Try the test and activities again – can you do more this time?

4 Programming: The Hungry Parrot

You will learn

→ how to use conditional loops and counter loops to control the movement of a sprite

→ how to make changes to a program to meet a requirement

→ how to use x and y coordinates to set a position.

In Unit 3 you learned how to use counter loops and conditional loops. In this unit you will use your new skills to make a simple computer game. In the game, a hungry parrot chases an apple. You will use coordinates to set the positions of the parrot and the apple on the screen. Then you will explore how different types of loop change the game.

Talk about...

In this unit you will make two versions of a computer game. In the first version the result depends on chance. In the second version the result depends on user skill. Most people think that games of skill are more fun to play. What do you think? What skills do you use in the games you like best? Think about all the games you play, not just computer games.

Did you know?

You can identify any point on the surface of Earth using just two numbers. These numbers are called latitude and longitude. Latitude tells you how far North or South (starting from the Equator). Longitude tells you how far East or West (starting from the Prime Meridian).

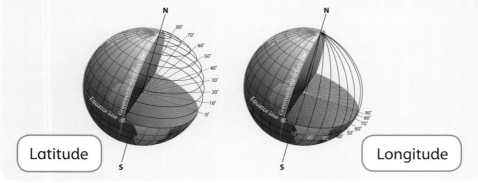

Latitude   Longitude

Learning outcomes: Adapt a program to meet a new requirement

Class activity

In this activity you will use number coordinates to play 'Treasure hunt'.

Draw a map of a deserted island. Add features such as trees, mountains and lakes. Use a ruler to draw a grid of rows and columns over the island. Number the columns and rows.

Each square is identified by an *x* coordinate (the number of the column) and a *y* coordinate (the number of the row). Decide where the treasure is. Write down the *x* and *y* coordinates of the square, but don't show your partner.

Challenge your partner to a game. Your partner guesses where the treasure is. If they are wrong, cross out that square. Continue until they find the right square. Now you can swap. You will try to find the treasure in your partner's island.

To make the game more interesting, include a hidden danger such as a deadly scorpion. If your partner chooses that square, they are out of the game.

> coordinates   *x* coordinate
> *y* coordinate   starting event
> costume   degree
> answer block   'go to' block

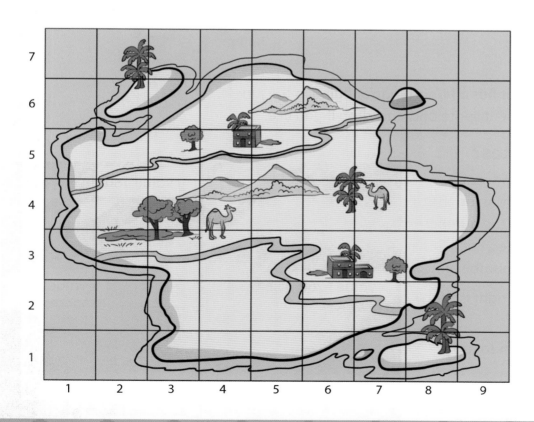

In this lesson

You will learn:

→ how to use coordinates to position a sprite on the screen.

Spiral back

In this lesson you will start to create a computer game. You have already learned how to choose a sprite and a backdrop. This page will remind you of what you have learned. If you have never used Scratch to control a sprite, look back at Student Book 4 before you start this unit.

Choose the sprite and backdrop

Open the Scratch website. The starting screen shows a cat sprite on a white backdrop. At the bottom right of the screen, there are buttons to add a new sprite and a new backdrop.

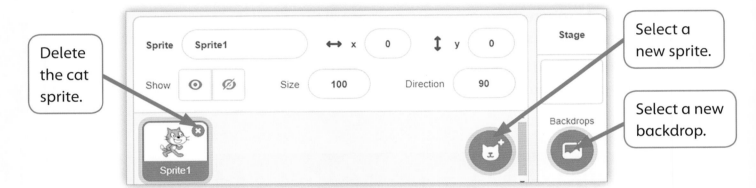

Delete the cat sprite.

Select a new sprite.

Select a new backdrop.

The game shown in this unit has a hungry parrot flying in the jungle. But you can choose a different sprite and backdrop if you like.

What are coordinates?

The area where the sprite moves is called the stage. Every position on the stage has a number value. The number values are called coordinates. Each **coordinate** point has two numbers:

● The position from left to right is the **x coordinate**.

● The position from bottom to top is the **y coordinate**.

The coordinates can be positive or negative numbers. The centre of the stage has *x* value 0 and *y* value 0.

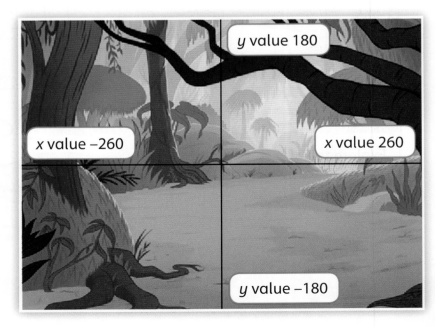

y value 180

x value −260

x value 260

y value −180

Set the starting values

Click on the sprite to change its size and position.

- The parrot sprite is too big so change the size from 100 to 50. That makes it half the size.

- Put the parrot at the left side of the screen. Change the *x* coordinate to –200 and the *y* coordinate to 0.

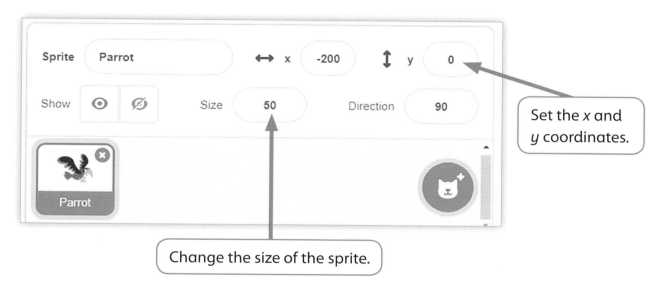

Set the *x* and *y* coordinates.

Change the size of the sprite.

Your screen is ready. Now you can start writing the program.

 Activity

Prepare a stage with a sprite and a backdrop.

Change the size and position of the sprite.

Save your file.

Extra challenge

Explore the number values for different positions on the screen. Drag the sprite to a new place on the stage. Look below the stage to see the *x* and *y* values for the new position.

Think again What are the *x* and *y* values of the top left corner of the stage?

In this lesson

You will learn:

→ how to write a script to move the sprite on the stage.

Start the program

Every program needs a **starting event**. The starting event is how the user makes the program start. For your game you will use the green flag button to start the program.

● Look at the yellow 'Events' blocks.

● Choose the green flag event block and drag it onto the stage.

Next set the starting position of the parrot.

● Look at the blue 'Motion' blocks.

● Find the 'go to' block. It says 'go to x: … y: …'. There is space to enter x and y coordinates.

● Put this block into the program.

● Set the x and y coordinates for the parrot to x = –200, y = 0.

Every time the program starts, the parrot will go to this position.

The program so far is shown in the top picture opposite.

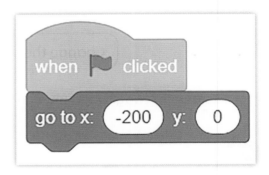

Move the sprite

The blue 'Motion' blocks make the sprite move. Find the 'move 10 steps' block. Add this to the program and then run the program.

The parrot doesn't move very far. To make it move further, put the 'move 10 steps' block inside a counter loop. The program so far is shown opposite.

The move block is repeated 10 times. When you run the program, the parrot moves further.

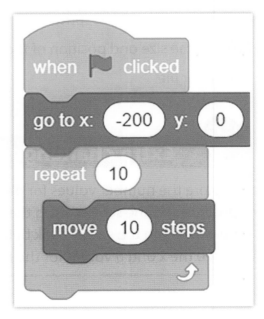

Flap the wings

To make the game more fun you will make the parrot flap its wings. The different 'Looks' for a sprite are called **costumes**. For the parrot these are different wing positions.

You will also make the sprite pause for a fraction of a second after each flap. That makes the movement more realistic.

The new blocks you will need are shown opposite. Make sure you change the 'wait' value to 0.2 (two tenths of a second).

Put the blocks inside the loop.

If you have chosen a different sprite, the costume change will look different. But it will still be fun to try.

 **Activity**

Write a program to move the sprite as shown in this lesson.

Run the program to make sure it works.

Save the file.

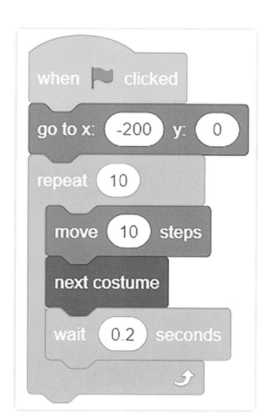

 Extra challenge

The program blocks in your program have numbers in them:

- the number of steps
- the number of repeats
- the number of seconds to wait between wing flaps.

Change these values and see how your changes affect the program.

Think again This program uses a loop. What kind of loop is it? What is the exit condition?

In this lesson

You will learn:

→ how to make a program with two sprites.

Give the parrot an apple

In this game the parrot is hungry. You will help the parrot find food to eat. You will make a program so the apple appears at a random place in front of the parrot.

Use the skills you have already learned to add an apple sprite to the program. Set the size to 50.

Move the apple

Now you will make a short program to control the apple sprite.

The starting event is the green flag.

The new program only needs one more block. Use the 'go to' block to move the sprite to an x and y coordinate.

Set the x and y values to 0 and fit the two blocks together.

The program looks like this.

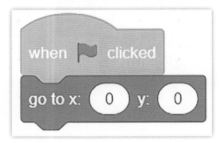

Make x random

Now you will make the x coordinate a random value. That means the block will move to a random place in front of the parrot.

Here is the block that makes a random value.

This block makes a random number from 1 to 10. But you will change it.

- The smallest possible value for the *x* coordinate is −260.
- The biggest possible value for the *x* coordinate is 260.

Type these numbers in the 'random' block.

Put the 'random' block into the program. The completed program looks like this.

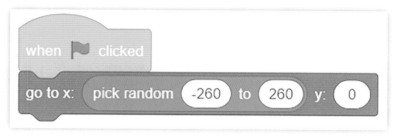

Run the program

When you run the program, the parrot flies towards the apple. But the position of the apple is random. So the parrot does not always reach the apple. Sometimes it goes past it.

 **Activity**

Add a second sprite (for example, an apple) as shown in this lesson. Make a program to control the new sprite. Run the program to make sure it works. Save the file.

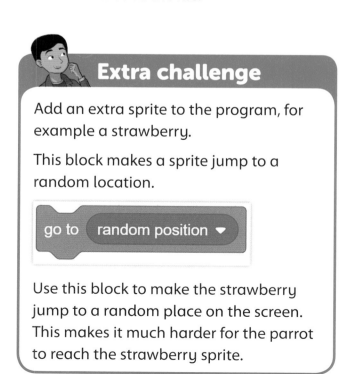 **Extra challenge**

Add an extra sprite to the program, for example a strawberry.

This block makes a sprite jump to a random location.

```
go to  random position ▼
```

Use this block to make the strawberry jump to a random place on the screen. This makes it much harder for the parrot to reach the strawberry sprite.

Think again

The *x* coordinate of the apple is any random value between −260 and 260.

a What does *x* coordinate mean?

b What does random mean?

c What other value is used with the *x* coordinate to set the position of a sprite?

In this lesson

You will learn:

→ how to use 'if… else' to control the output of a program.

If… else

You will change the program to show if the parrot has reached its dinner. You will add more commands to the program.

Click on the parrot sprite. You will use the 'if… else' block. You have used this block before in Unit 3. Add it to the program. It comes after the loop, when the parrot has finished moving.

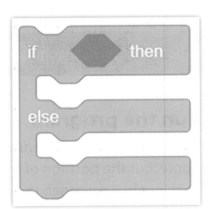

Sensing

The light blue 'Sensing' blocks are used by the computer to 'sense' if an event happens. One of these blocks will sense if the parrot is touching the apple. Here is the block. Use the drop-down menu to choose 'Apple'.

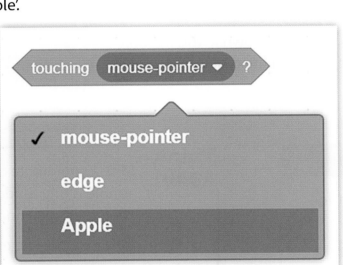

This block makes a test. If the parrot touches the apple, the test is True. If the parrot does not touch the apple, the test is False.

This sensing block goes into the program at the top of the 'if… else' block.

Complete the program

Finally, put 'say' blocks into the program.

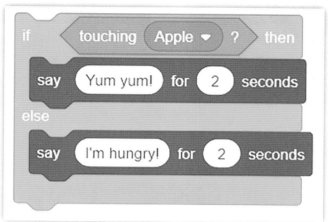

- If the parrot touches the apple, the parrot says "Yum yum!"

- Else, the parrot says "I'm hungry!"

Here is the program with these changes.

Run the program and you will see if the parrot gets its dinner.

 Activity

Add the 'if… else' section shown in this lesson. Run the program to make sure it works. Save your file.

 Extra challenge

If you have not done this already, add a strawberry to the game. If the parrot touches the strawberry, the parrot says "I like this dinner!"

Hint: You must put the test about the strawberry before the test about the apple.

 Be creative

Draw an idea for a similar game. Instead of a parrot flying to eat an apple, you can choose a different backdrop and different sprites.

 Explore more

Play the parrot game several times. Keep a tally of how often the parrot reaches the apple. What is the percentage?

In this lesson

You will learn:

→ how to use input values to control a counter loop.

Use your skill

The game you have made so far is not very good. The user does not need to use skill to play the game. The parrot might reach the apple or it might not. The result is random. Now you will change the program so the parrot asks you how many flaps to take.

After you type a number (for example, 3), the parrot will flap its wings that many times. It will move forwards that many times.

If you input the right number, the parrot will get the apple. You must use your skill to choose the right number.

Ask a question

You used the 'ask' block in Unit 3. Find this block and change the question to 'How many times shall I flap my wings?'

Before you can insert a block into a program, you have to pull the blocks apart. Put the new block into the program before the loop. Then fit the blocks back together again.

The start of the program is shown in the top picture.

Enter a number

The user can type an answer to the question.

You learned in Unit 3 that the user's answer to a question is stored by the computer. The answer is stored as a light blue 'answer' block. You will put this block into the counter loop. The loop will repeat that number of times.

For example, if you type 6 the loop will repeat six times. Run the program to see what happens.

Multiply by 2

The program is still not quite right. If you enter 6, the parrot flaps its wings three times. That is because each flap of the wings uses two loops:

- one loop to move the wings up
- one loop to move the wings down.

So you need to loop two times for every flap. You will use the multiplication operator *. You used this operator in Unit 3. You will multiply the user's answer by 2.

Put this operator into the counter loop. Now the parrot will flap its wings the right number of times.

The finished game

The completed program is shown opposite. Check your work against this image to make sure you get everything right.

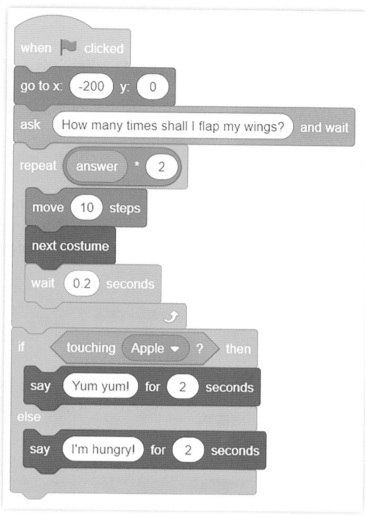

Complete the parrot game using the program shown in this lesson. Run the program to make sure it works. Save your file.

Think again Make a plan for the parrot game. Show the inputs, outputs and processes.

Extra challenge

Start a new file. Create a new version of this game using different sprites and a different backdrop. Can you create the whole program without checking in this book?

In this lesson

You will learn:

→ how to use a conditional loop in a game

→ how to work independently to make a game.

I got my dinner!

A new game

In this lesson you will make a new game called Chase Your Dinner! You will work independently and use the images to help you. Only start this project if you have completed all the other lessons in this unit.

Start a new program. Choose a backdrop. Add two sprites:

● One sprite is the food.

● The other sprite will chase the food.

You can use the parrot and apple again if you like. The example game in this lesson uses a robot and a muffin.

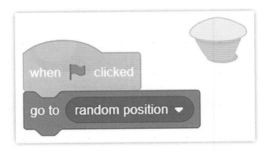

Position the food

Make a simple program for the food sprite so that it moves to a random position on the screen.

Position the chaser

The other sprite chases the food. It is the chaser. Start a program for the chaser. Set the x and y coordinates and the direction as shown in this picture.

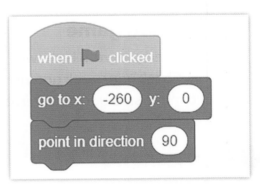

How many degrees?

Angles are measured in **degrees**. A right-angle is 90 degrees. This program will ask the user to type a number of degrees. The chaser will turn that many degrees.

Use these blocks.

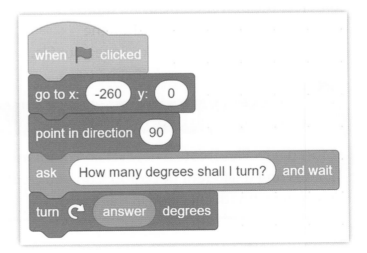

Keep moving

The picture opposite shows a conditional loop. The loop will repeat until the chaser touches the food.

Inside the loop there are two commands: a command to keep moving forward, and a command to bounce off the edge of the screen. This means the chaser sprite will keep moving until it gets the food.

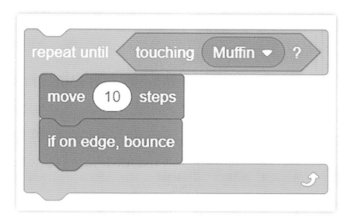

Finishing touches

You can add some finishing touches to the game.

- Inside the loop, add commands to change the costume and to wait 0.2 seconds. This will make the movement more realistic.

- After the loop is finished, the chaser has caught the food. Make the chaser say something like "I got my dinner!"

The finished game

The completed program looks like this. Check your work against this image.

 **Activity**

Make a new game like the one shown in this lesson. Run the program to make sure it works. Save your file.

 Extra challenge

Change the program so that both the food and the chaser move about on the screen. That makes it harder for the chaser to catch the food.

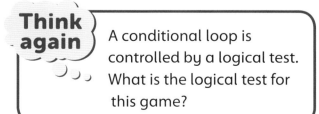

Think again

A conditional loop is controlled by a logical test. What is the logical test for this game?

You have learned

→ how to use conditional and counter loops to control the movement of a sprite

→ how to make changes to a program to meet a requirement

→ how to use *x* and *y* coordinates to set a position.

Test

Zara is making a Scratch program. The program will control the movement of a snow hare.

The hare moves forward 25 steps.

1 Zara wants the hare to keep moving and never stop as long as the program is running. Which block will make this happen? Draw or name it.

2 Zara wants to change the program so that the hare repeats the movement 10 times. Which block will make this happen? Draw or name it.

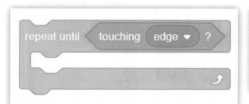

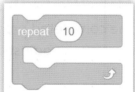

3 Zara wants the user to decide how far the hare will move. Which group of blocks will make this happen? Draw or name them.

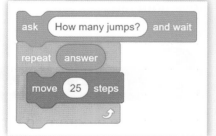

 **Activities**

Jas has created a program that makes a spaceship move about in space. It has a forever loop. Here is the program.

1 Make this program and run it.

2 Change the program so that the sprite moves 6 steps in each loop.

3 Change the program so that the loop repeats 100 times then stops.

4 Change the program so that instead of a counter loop, the program loops until the sprite touches the mouse pointer.

Self-evaluation

- I answered test question 1.

- I completed activity 1. I made a program that works.

- I answered test questions 1 and 2.

- I completed activities 1–3. I made the program and then I made some changes to it.

- I answered all the test questions.

- I completed all of the activities.

Re-read any parts of the unit you feel unsure about. Try the test and activities again – can you do more this time?

5 Multimedia: Illustrating a recipe card

You will learn

→ how to plan a photo shoot for a project

→ how to take good photos using a digital camera

→ how to improve your photos using a computer

→ how to combine photos in a document to create an illustration to go with your text.

Talk about...

What are your ideas for photos to go with recipes? What should they show?

Digital photography is a great way to create illustrations for your projects. Digital cameras are built into many modern devices. You can connect these devices to computers or share the photos online so that you can use them in documents. You can also edit your photos to improve them.

The history of photography

1826

Film cameras: The first cameras to use film were invented over 100 years ago. The 'Brownie' camera was cheap and easy to use. Now anyone could be a photographer.

1888

Plate cameras: The first photographs were made about 200 years ago. The early cameras made images on a metal plate. The images they made were called Daguerreotypes.

Learning outcomes: Make and share images to suit an audience and a purpose; Amend an image to increase its impact

In this unit you are going to make, edit and combine **digital photos** to illustrate a recipe. A digital photo is made with a camera that stores images as digital data.

digital photo
photo shoot
composition   subject
USB   storyboard   crop
tag

 Class activity

1 What makes a good photo in a book or magazine? Choose a photo you like and write down all the reasons why it is a good photo.

First think about the photo itself. Then think about how it works together with text on the page.

2 Make a list of devices that have built-in cameras. How many are there in your home?

Did you know?

Cameras have changed a lot since 1826. Researchers estimate that around 1.2 trillion (1,200,000,000,000) photos are now taken every year. Most people use a smartphone to take photos.

Cameras everywhere: Today, digital cameras are built into many other devices. Most smartphones, laptop computers and tablets have a built-in digital camera.

1990s

2000s

Digital cameras: In the 1990s digital cameras became more popular than film cameras. Digital cameras work together with computers. The cameras store photos as files. You can use a computer to store and change images.

In this lesson

You will learn:

→ how to plan a photo shoot for a recipe page

→ how to vary image types to make a document more interesting and useful.

Spiral back

In Student Books 2 and 3 you learned how to use images and text in a document. In this unit you will learn more about making images to go with your text. You will learn how combine images and text in different ways to make your documents more exciting and useful.

What is a photo shoot?

When professional photographers take photos for a project, they call it a **photo shoot**. They always plan a photo shoot carefully so that they get all the right photos for the project. You need to plan your photo shoot, too.

Ideas for your photo shoot

A good way to get ideas is to look at how other people have used photos to illustrate their work.

To get ideas for your recipe photo shoot you could look at:

● recipe books at school or at home

● recipe websites and food blogs on the internet.

Make a plan

1 First you need to choose a recipe.

   ● What steps are there in the recipe?

   ● Which are the most important steps?

   ● Which steps will make the best photos?

2 Try to use a variety of types of photos to make the recipe look more interesting. You can use:

   ● **different compositions:** close-ups and wide shots

   ● **different angles:** photos taken from above, the side or below

   ● **props:** such as kitchen tools

   ● **actions:** show a person, or just their hands, doing some of the steps in the recipe.

This photo shows a person using a prop and performing an action in the recipe.

3 Use a **storyboard** to help you decide what photos to include. A storyboard is a series of simple drawings that show the order of the photos. A storyboard also shows what will be in each photo.

Your storyboard will help you decide what ingredients, props and actions will be in the photos.

 **Activity**

Choose a recipe.

Choose which steps of the recipe to photograph. Choose no more than six steps.

Draw a storyboard that shows all the photos you need to take.

 Extra challenge

Imagine you are a picture editor. It is your job to tell the photographer which photos they need to take. You need to give instructions about: location, people, design and colours. Write your instructions to the photographer on your storyboard.

 **Explore more**

Think about the props or materials you need for your photo shoot. For example, a bowl or a picture of ingredients. Find the props you need and bring them to the next lesson.

In this lesson

You will learn:

→ how to take photos using your digital camera

→ how to compose a picture

→ how to focus your camera on a subject

→ how to use light to make your photo look good.

Composing a photo

Every photo has a **subject**. The subject is the main thing you want to show. You can decide where in your photo to place your subject. In many photos the subject is in the centre of the image. You can put your subject in other places to make a more interesting **composition**.

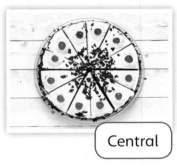
Central

Focusing on your subject

When your photo is in focus it looks clear and not blurred. Most modern cameras have **autofocus**. Autofocus measures the distance between the camera and the subject and sets the correct focus for the image.

You can use the camera's viewfinder or screen to help you focus on the subject. When you use a smartphone you can use the touchscreen to tell the camera where to focus.

Rule of thirds

Off-centre

Lighting your photo

Your camera can measure and control the **exposure** of each photo. The exposure is the amount of light that reaches the sensor to make each photo.

The camera can set the **shutter speed** to control the length of time light is captured by the sensor. If the shutter speed is too low the photo will become blurred when the subject moves.

The camera can control the sensor's sensitivity to light. The setting is sometimes called **ISO**. When the ISO setting is increased, the camera can take photos with less light. If the ISO is increased too far, the photo can look grainy and speckled.

Most cameras have a built-in flash. Using the flash is not always the best way to light photos. The flash can make the photo overexposed. Your close-up photos might have dark edges and a very bright centre.

Low light can make photos blurred. Sometimes this can look good.

Activity

Use a camera or smartphone to take photos that match your storyboard. Follow the instructions you wrote in the last lesson. Use different compositions and different lighting. Take photos with and without flash.

Now compare your photos. Which one looks best? Explain why you think so.

Compare your best photo with your classmates' best photos. Talk about the differences between the photos.

The speckles that appear on the photo are called **noise**.

Extra challenge

Find the manual settings menu on your camera or smartphone. Change the shutter speed and ISO settings and compare the photos you take. How do the changes affect the photos?

This photo is overexposed.

Explore more

Think of a theme such as 'celebration' or 'happiness' or your favourite colour. Use your camera to take photos of subjects around your home. Try different compositions and lighting. Save your favourite photos.

5 Multimedia: Illustrating a recipe card

In this lesson

You will learn:

→ how to connect your digital camera to copy photos to a computer

→ how to share your photos using cloud storage

→ how use albums to organise your photos.

Mini USB

Standard USB

Micro USB

Transferring your photos

To use your photos in a document or other project, you must first transfer them from your digital camera or smartphone to the computer. You can do this by connecting the camera to the computer. You can also transfer your photos via the internet.

Connect a camera to your computer

You can use a **USB** cable to connect most digital devices to your computer. There are different sizes of USB.

Make sure you have the correct cable. Your computer usually has a standard USB plug socket, but your camera or phone may have a smaller socket.

Connect your camera or smartphone to your computer. Insert the correct USB plug in each device. You will see a dialogue box.

You can use the Photos application to import the photos. Click on 'Import Photos and Videos'.

HTC One M9

Choose what to do with this device.

Import photos and videos
Photos

Your computer will find the photo files on the camera. Tick the files you want to import. Click 'Import selected'. The computer will copy your photos to the 'Pictures' folder on the computer.

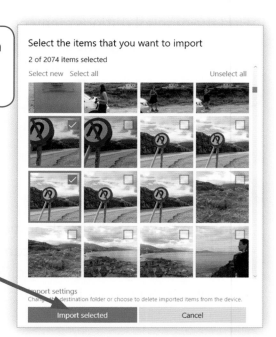

Select the items that you want to import
2 of 2074 items selected
Select new   Select all   Unselect all

Import settings
Change the destination folder or choose to delete imported items from the device.

Import selected   Cancel

Share your photos using cloud storage

If you have taken your photos on a smartphone, tablet or internet-ready camera, you can use cloud storage to store your photo files. Your computer can then access the files via the internet.

There are many different cloud storage services, such as OneDrive, Google Photos, iCloud and Dropbox. Most cloud storage services allow you to see and work with your photos on a computer.

Organise your photos in albums

Photos are usually stored in date order on your computer. You can put photos into albums to help you find them again later.

You can add images to an album in the Photos application. You can create new albums for different themes or projects.

Remember: Before you connect a device to your computer, always ask permission from the device's owner **and** from the computer's owner.

Activity

Transfer your photos to your computer – use a USB cable or cloud storage.

In the Photos application, choose the photos you want for your recipe.

Create an album for your recipe.

Put all your chosen photos into your new album.

Extra challenge

Can you think of other ways of sharing photos between devices? Write down your suggestions. Write down the advantages and disadvantages of each of your suggestions.

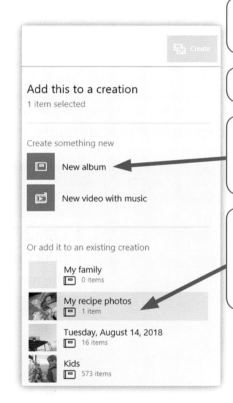

1 Select one or more images.

2 Select 'Add to…'

3 **Either** create a new album for your project

or add the photo to an album you have already created.

Think again Why do you need to ask permission before you connect a device to a computer?

In this lesson

You will learn:

→ how to use software to improve your digital photos

→ how to use filters to change the look of a photo

→ how to make manual changes to control the look and shape of a photo.

Picture editing software

Sometimes digital photos are not perfect. You can use picture editing software to improve the exposure, colour and composition. Picture editing software is available on computers and other devices such as smartphones and tablets.

Use filters

Filters are a quick and easy way to change a photo. Many picture editing applications provide filters.

To edit your photos in the Windows Photos application, choose the 'Edit' function.

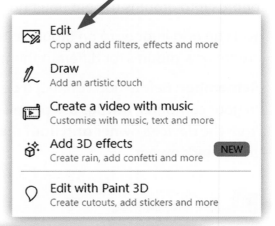

Edit
Crop and add filters, effects and more

Draw
Add an artistic touch

Create a video with music
Customise with music, text and more

Add 3D effects NEW
Create rain, add confetti and more

Edit with Paint 3D
Create cutouts, add stickers and more

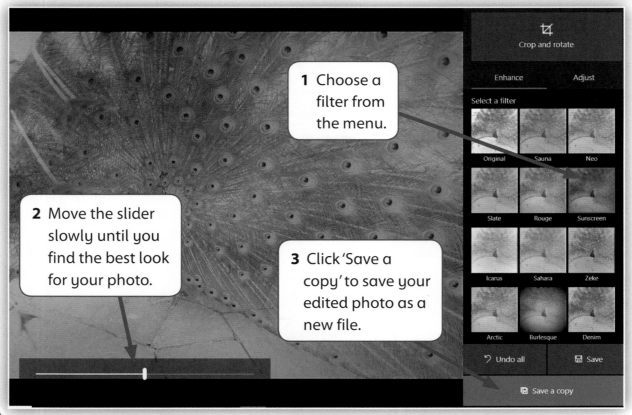

1 Choose a filter from the menu.

2 Move the slider slowly until you find the best look for your photo.

3 Click 'Save a copy' to save your edited photo as a new file.

Make manual changes to your photos

Always follow the correct order when you edit your photos manually. This is called the **workflow**.

In the Microsoft Photos application the 'Adjust' menu is organised in the correct order.

1 Exposure: Always start with the 'Light' setting. This changes the exposure of your photo. If the photo is too dark or too bright you can move the 'Light' slider slowly to reduce the exposure.

2 Colour: Next use the 'Colour' slider. Move the slider to the left to make the photo less colourful, until it is **monochrome**. Monochrome photos use the tones of just one colour, such as tones of grey. Move the slider to the right to make the colours stronger and brighter.

3 Composition: Finally, you can crop your photo to improve the composition.

- Drag the handles to resize the box. This will be the **frame** of your edited photo.

- Click inside the box to move the image around inside your new frame.

- Click on 'Done' to cut away the parts of the photo that are outside the box.

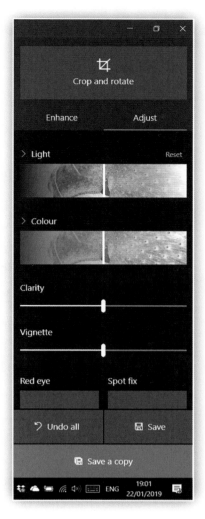

 **Activity**

Decide what edits to make to your photos. Use your storyboard and written instructions to help you decide.

Use the exposure and colour settings to improve your photo. Use the crop tool to highlight the main subject in each image.

Save your edited photos.

 Extra challenge

Explore the other functions in the 'Adjust' menu. Can you improve your photos by using the 'Clarity', 'Vignette' and 'Rotate' functions? Try each function and describe what it does.

 **Think again**

What are the advantages of using filters? What are the advantages of making manual changes to your photos?

In this lesson

You will learn:

→ how to use spot fix and cloning tools in photo editing software.

What is retouching?

Photo editing software provides powerful tools to change photos. Sometimes you might want to remove something from a photo. Sometimes you might want to add something. Making changes like these is called **retouching**.

Use the spot fix brush to edit small areas

The 'Spot fix' tool can remove small marks on a photo. The spot fix tool **samples** pixels around the area you want to retouch. It copies the area around the cursor. It uses this information to paint over the area you want to retouch.

1 Zoom in closely to the area you want to fix. Click on the 'Spot fix' button.

2 Move the cursor to the area you want to fix and click. Move the cursor along and click again until the area is fixed.

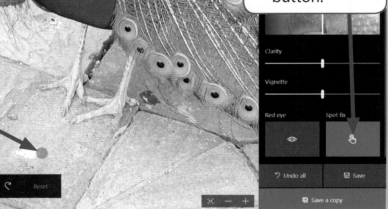

The white mark on the floor has been removed.

Use the clone tool to make bigger changes

Some photo editing software provides a clone tool. The clone tool uses pixels from one part of the image to paint over pixels in another part. You can use cloning to remove whole objects in your photo.

This example uses the 'Clone Stamp' tool in the GIMP application. Here is how to remove the leaf at the side of the pan in this photo.

1 Zoom in to the area you want to fix. Select the 'Clone Stamp' tool.

2 Choose the brush size from the menu on the right, to match the area you want to fix.

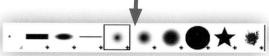

3 Move the cursor to a part of the photo you want to sample. Hold down CTRL and click. Move the cursor to the area you want to fix. Click and drag the mouse to paint over the area with the sampled pixels.

 Activity

Look at the photos you have been working on in this unit. Find any areas that need retouching.

Decide what editing tool to use to retouch your images.

Use your chosen tool to retouch the images.

Save your images.

Extra challenge

Compare your retouched images to the originals. Write down the ways in which they have changed. Have the changes made the photos better or worse? Explain why.

Digital citizen of the future

Many years ago, people said: "The camera never lies."

Today, it is easy to change photos to make the subject look better. You can use filters to make a photo brighter. You can crop a photo to remove things. You can use cloning to make things disappear.

When you look at photos in magazines and adverts, ask yourself: "How might this image have been changed?"

Think again

Find a photo in a magazine or an advert. How might this image have been changed?

In this lesson

You will learn:

→ how to add your photos to a text document

→ how to arrange photos so that they fit together well with your text.

How to put a photo together with text

Use the 'Wrap Text' menu to change how text fits around a photo. You can also move, resize and rotate the photo.

> Choose how the text will wrap around the photo. Then drag the photo to a new place on the page. Try different text-wrapping options to see which works best.

> Use the handles to make the photo bigger or smaller. Use the corner handles to avoid stretching or squashing your photo.

> Use the rotation handle at the top of the photo. Turn the photo so it is at an angle.

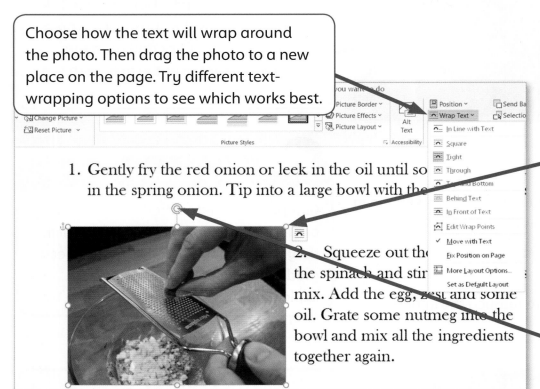

How to group photos together

Making a collage

You can overlap images to make an interesting collage. This can be useful for making a cover illustration. Use the 'Arrange' functions on the 'Picture Tools' ribbon.

Use the mouse to arrange photos so that they overlap. You can click on a photo and use the 'Bring Forward' and 'Send Backward' buttons to change which photo is at the front. You now have a stack of photos.

Grouping photos

Select all the images in your stack: hold down the 'Shift' key as you click on the photos one by one. Then click the 'Group' button to make your stack into a single image.

> Use these buttons to change the order of images.

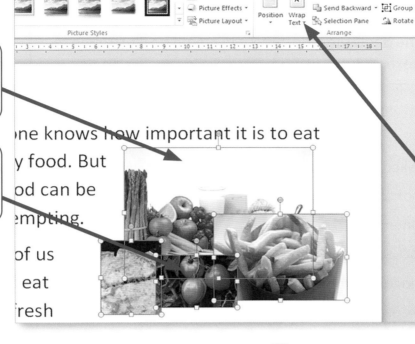

> Use the 'Group' button to make all the selected photos into one image.

> This photo is behind all the others.

> This photo is in front of the others.

> Choose an option from the 'Wrap Text' menu.

Activity

Open your recipe document in Microsoft Word.

Add your recipe text.

Insert the images you want to use to illustrate your recipe.

Move and resize the photos to create a one-page document for your recipe.

Extra challenge

Create a cover page for your recipe. Use some of your recipe images and create a collage. Add the recipe name at the top of the page.

Think again

What do you need to think about when you put words and images together on a page? How do words and images work best together?

Be creative

Use the 'Picture Styles' menu to change the look of your photos. If you are working with an image stack, ungroup the images and change each photo separately. Then group them again.

Explore more functions in the 'Adjust' menu of the 'Picture Tools' ribbon. Try the 'Color' and 'Artistic Effects' menus.

Check what you know

You have learned

→ how to plan a photo shoot for a project

→ how to take good photos using a digital camera

→ how to improve your photos using a computer

→ how to combine photos in a document to create an illustration to go with your text.

Test

You have been asked to plan a photo shoot for one of these events:

- making a cup of coffee
- going to the cinema
- launching a rocket to the moon.

1 Sketch an idea for one photo that you could take.

2 Draw up to six pictures in your storyboard.

3 Write a caption for each picture in the storyboard. It should explain what the photo will show and why you have chosen it.

 **Activities**

In this unit you have created a range of digital photos. For these activities, you will present and discuss one of your photos.

1. Select one of the photos you created. Put this photo into a document. Add a note saying what the image shows.

2. Explain one way that you have edited or changed the photo. If possible, show the photo before and after you made the change.

3. Explain why you made the change. How did you use the image in your work?

Before editing   After editing

Self-evaluation

- I answered test question 1.
- I completed activity 1. I put a photo into a document.
- I answered test questions 1 and 2.
- I completed activities 1 and 2. I explained how I changed the photo.
- I answered all the test questions.
- I completed all of the activities.

Re-read any parts of the unit you feel unsure about. Try the test and activities again – can you do more this time?

6 Numbers and data: My pizza snack bar

You will learn

→ how to store text and number values using a spreadsheet

→ how to use spreadsheet formulas to calculate results

→ how to use a spreadsheet to help manage a business

→ how to explore the effect of changes to values.

A spreadsheet is a type of software application. Spreadsheets are used to process numbers.

Businesses use spreadsheets to manage their accounts. Spreadsheets can store information about a business's income – this is the money that a business receives. Spreadsheets can also store information about a business's costs – this is the money that a business spends. A business needs to understand its costs and its income to make a profit.

In this unit you will use a spreadsheet to record the costs and income of a snack bar that sells pizza slices and desserts.

Learning outcomes: Use a spreadsheet to answer questions by finding out what happens when numbers change

Class activity

In a small group, talk about your ideas for a business. What would your business sell? Think about your costs and your income. Here are some ideas:

Cafe: What recipes would you make? Choose a recipe you like.

- How much would it cost to make this recipe?
- How many portions would your recipe make?
- How much would you sell each portion for?

Bead jewellery: What jewellery would you make? Think of a design for a bracelet or necklace.

- How much would the materials cost?
- How long would it take to make?
- How much would you sell the jewellery for?

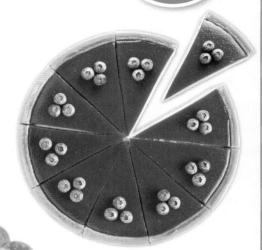

format   formula
profit   right-click
mathematical model
income   costs

Did you know?

The spreadsheets used in big businesses can be very large and complicated. This means that the spreadsheets sometimes contain errors.

A huge spreadsheet error happened at a company called Fidelity Magellan. An accountant forgot to put a negative sign in a spreadsheet formula. Instead of showing a loss of $1.3 billion, the spreadsheet showed a gain. Nobody noticed until the company's profit was $2.6 billion less than the spreadsheet predicted.

You must use spreadsheets carefully. You must check your work for errors.

Talk about...

What other business ideas have you got? Talk about the costs you need to record for this business.

6 Numbers and data: My pizza snack bar

In this lesson

You will learn:

→ how to enter values into a spreadsheet

→ how to format values as currency.

Spiral back

In Student Book 4 you learned how to use spreadsheet functions and formulas. In this unit you will learn how to use the results of formulas to help a business make decisions about its products.

Values and labels

Imagine that you own a pizza snack bar. The snack bar sells slices of pizza and desserts to customers. In this lesson you will use a spreadsheet to calculate the costs and the income of your pizza snack bar.

Spreadsheets contain two types of data:

● **Values** – these are numbers. Values are used in calculations.

● **Labels** – these are text. Labels are used to show what the values mean, so the spreadsheet is easier to understand.

Look at the spreadsheet 'My pizza snack bar'. The first worksheet lists the ingredients for a recipe called 'Pizza Napoli'. It only has labels. In this lesson you will enter the costs of the ingredients.

How to enter data into a spreadsheet

Click on a cell with the pointer to select it.

Type the data you want to enter. Then press 'Enter' to add the data to the cell.

Now the spreadsheet includes labels and values. They are shown in different ways.

● Labels are **left-aligned** – they are at the left of the cell.

● Values are **right-aligned** – they are at the right of the cell.

A spreadsheet is divided into cells. In this spreadsheet cell C4 is selected.

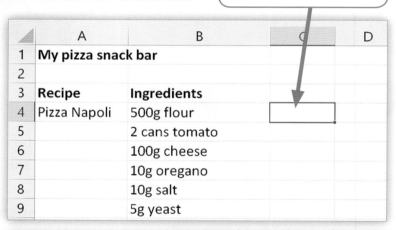

	A	B	C	D
1	**My pizza snack bar**			
2				
3	**Recipe**	**Ingredients**		
4	Pizza Napoli	500g flour		
5		2 cans tomato		
6		100g cheese		
7		10g oregano		
8		10g salt		
9		5g yeast		

	A	B	C	D
1	**My pizza snack bar**			
2				
3	**Recipe**	**Ingredients**		
4	Pizza Napoli	500g flour	0.75	
5		2 cans tomato	1.2	
6		100g cheese	1	
7		10g oregano	0.05	
8		10g salt	0.01	
9		5g yeast	0.1	
10				

You can also change the **format** of the values. Format means the style of something or how it is organised. In a spreadsheet use the 'Number Format' to choose the way values are shown. There are many different number formats such as decimal number, date and time, percentage, currency.

The currency format shows values as amounts of money. In this lesson you will change the costs of the ingredients to currency values.

Change cells to a currency format

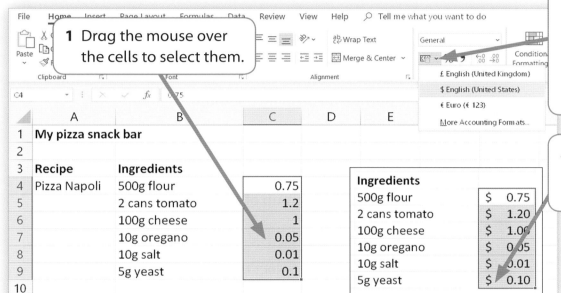

1 Drag the mouse over the cells to select them.

2 Click this button to choose a currency format.

This spreadsheet uses dollars, but you can choose another currency.

3 The selected cells change to currency.

Activity

Open the spreadsheet 'My pizza snack bar'.

On the 'Pizza Napoli' worksheet, enter the number values shown in this lesson.

Format the values as currency.

Save your work.

Extra challenge

Your spreadsheet only shows the costs of the ingredients for your recipe. A real snack bar has lots of other costs too. Write down the other costs you can think of.

Think again

To make a profit, a business must keep costs low and income high.

- How do businesses try to keep costs low?

- How do businesses try to keep income high?

- Think of a successful business where you live. What do you think makes the business successful?

In this lesson

You will learn:

→ how to use the AutoSum function to add up a column of values

→ how to use a formula to calculate results.

Calculate the cost of one portion of pizza

You will use two spreadsheet functions to find out the cost of one portion of Pizza Napoli:

● AutoSum – add up the total cost of the recipe.

● A divide formula – find the cost of one portion by dividing the total cost of the recipe by the number of portions.

Use AutoSum

Sum is a mathematical term that means 'add a group of numbers together'. In a spreadsheet, AutoSum adds together a group of values. This is the AutoSum button.

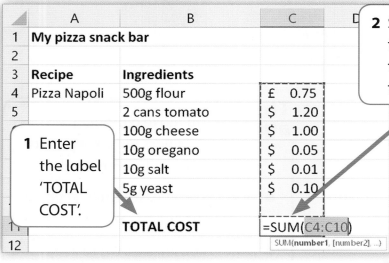

2 Select the cell where you want the total to appear. Make sure the cell is in the same column as your values. Click the AutoSum button.

1 Enter the label 'TOTAL COST'.

3 Press 'Enter'. The spreadsheet adds together the values in the highlighted cells.

Calculate the cost of one portion

In this example, one pizza makes eight portions. You can enter a different number if you want larger or smaller portions.

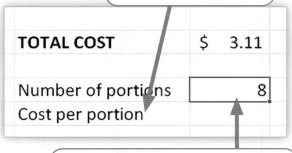

1 Enter these labels.

2 Enter the number of portions.

Now you will enter a **formula**. A formula is an instruction that tells the spreadsheet application to do a calculation. Every formula begins with an equals sign.

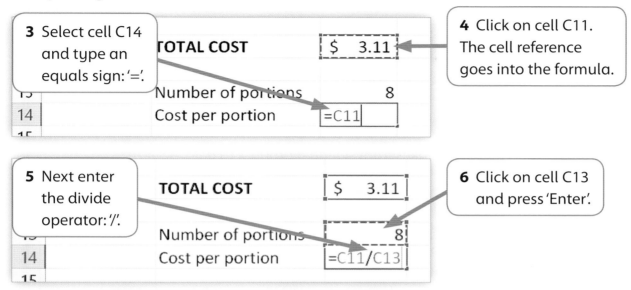

3 Select cell C14 and type an equals sign: '='.

4 Click on cell C11. The cell reference goes into the formula.

TOTAL COST $ 3.11

Number of portions   8

Cost per portion   =C11

5 Next enter the divide operator: '/'.

6 Click on cell C13 and press 'Enter'.

TOTAL COST $ 3.11

Number of portions   8

Cost per portion   =C11/C13

The finished formula looks like this: =C11/C13

The formula means: 'the value in cell C11 divided by the value in cell C13'.

It is important to use **cell references** and not numbers in formulas. A cell reference tells the spreadsheet to take a value from a cell. If you change the value in the cell, the result of the formula changes too.

 **Activity**

Use the spreadsheet functions shown in this lesson to calculate the cost of making one portion of the Pizza Napoli recipe.

Save your work.

Think again

You have learned that changing the values in a spreadsheet changes the result of calculations. What other values can you see on your spreadsheet? What would happen if these values changed?

 Extra challenge

The number in cell C13 shows the number of portions. If you change this number, the cost of each portion changes too.

Try entering different values in this cell. What happens to the cost per portion if you make more portions from your recipe?

In this lesson

You will learn:

→ more ways of making spreadsheet formulas

→ how to use your spreadsheet to calculate business profits.

What is profit?

Profit is the money that a business makes from selling a product to a customer. Profit = income − costs.

In this lesson you will calculate the profit from selling one portion of pizza. First decide the selling price of one portion of pizza. To make a profit, the selling price must be more than the cost of the ingredients. In this example the price is $1.00. You can choose any value you like.

Prepare the spreadsheet structure

Enter more labels into the spreadsheet as shown in this picture.

13		Number of portions	8
14		Cost per portion	$ 0.39
15		Selling price	$ 1.00

> Enter the selling price for one portion. Format the value as currency.

Enter a spreadsheet formula to calculate profit

Select cell C17. The profit per portion will be shown in this cell. Now enter your formula.

1 Type an equals sign.

2 Select the cell with the selling price of one portion. Check that the cell reference has appeared in your formula in cell C17.

3 Type the subtract sign.

4 Select the cell with the cost per portion. Check that the cell reference has appeared in cell C17.

5 Press 'Enter'.

> You can also look at this box to check that your formula uses the correct cell references.

| SUM | ⋮ | ✕ ✓ *fx* | =C15-C14 |

10			
11		**TOTAL COST**	$ 3.11
12			
13		Number of portions	8
14		Cost per portion	$ 0.39
15		Selling price	$ 1.00
16			
17		**PROFIT PER PORTION**	=C15-C14
18			

Activities

1. Calculate the profit per portion of Pizza Napoli. Use the spreadsheet structure and formula shown in this lesson.

2. Your pizza snack bar also sells a dessert called Tiramisu Cake. Tiramisu is a famous Italian dessert.

19		
◀ ▶	**Pizza Napoli**	Tiramisu Cake ◀
Ready		

Click on this tab to open the worksheet for activity 2.

Use all the skills you have learned in this unit to calculate the profit per portion of Tiramisu Cake. Carry out these steps:

- Use AutoSum to add up the total cost of the ingredients.

- Enter the number of portions that each Tiramisu Cake recipe will make.

- Calculate the cost of one portion.

- Enter the selling price of one portion.

- Enter a formula to calculate the profit per portion.

Hint: Look back at the work you did in Lesson 6.2 for help with this activity.

	Recipe	Ingredients		
3	**Recipe**	**Ingredients**		
4	Tiramisu Cake	1000ml cream	$	2.50
5		500g cheese	$	5.00
6		150g sugar	$	0.50
7		600ml coffee	$	1.25
8		400g biscuit	$	1.00
9		50g chocolate	$	0.75
10				
11		**TOTAL COST**	$	11.00
12				
13		Number of portions		12
14		Cost per portion	$	0.92
15		Selling price	$	1.50
16				
17		**PROFIT PER PORTION**	$	0.58

Extra challenge

Remember that if you change the values, the results of a formula will also change. Try different values for:

- Number of portions
- Selling price.

Continue until you are happy that your pizza slices and cake portions are making a profit.

Think again Your pizza snack bar now sells pizza and dessert. What other products could it sell? What are the ingredients for these products? Write down your ideas.

In this lesson

You will learn:

→ how to create a new worksheet with labels and values

→ how to create formulas that use values from several worksheets

→ how to calculate summary data for a business.

In this lesson you will create a new worksheet in your spreadsheet file 'My pizza snack bar'. This worksheet will summarise the information from the worksheets 'Pizza Napoli' and 'Tiramisu Cake'.

Create a new worksheet

At the bottom of the spreadsheet application window, click on the + sign to create a new worksheet. Change the name of the new worksheet to 'My profits'.

The 'My profits' worksheet will show information about both your products.

Change the width of columns

Here is a suggested layout for the worksheet. Some of the labels are too long for the column width. When you enter these labels, they will also cover the cell to the right.

You can make the columns wider to fit the labels.

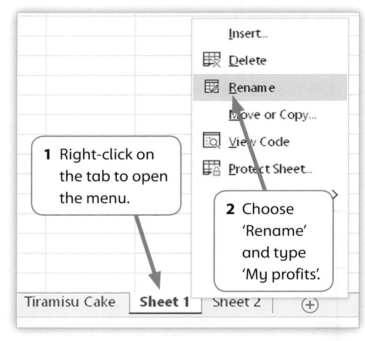

1 Right-click on the tab to open the menu.

2 Choose 'Rename' and type 'My profits'.

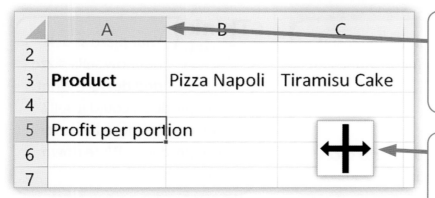

Select a cell in the column you want to make wider. Move the pointer to the right edge of the column.

When the pointer is in the correct place, it will change to look like this. Hold down the left mouse button and drag to make a column narrower or wider.

Insert cell references to other worksheets

The new worksheet will show the profit per portion for each product. It will take this information from the other two worksheets. To link the information, you will insert cell references.

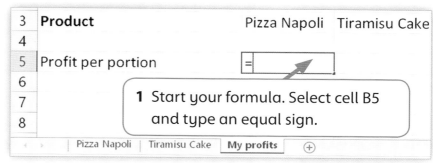

1 Start your formula. Select cell B5 and type an equal sign.

In this example you will insert a cell reference that links to the profit per portion for Pizza Napoli.

2 Click on the tab for the Pizza Napoli worksheet.

13	Number of portions		8
14	Cost per portion	$	0.39
15	Selling price	$	1.00
	PROFIT PER PORTION	$	0.61

3 Click on the cell that shows the profit per portion.

	A	B
3	**Product**	Pizza Napoli
4		
5	Profit per portion	$ 0.61
6		

B5 f_x ='Pizza Napoli'!C17

4 The cell reference includes the name of the worksheet.

Activity

Create a new worksheet called 'My profits'.

Add the labels shown in this lesson.

Change the column widths so that the labels fit.

Insert cell references to show the 'Profit per portion' for:

- Pizza Napoli
- Tiramisu Cake

Save your work.

Extra challenge

Change the values in the Pizza Napoli and Tiramisu Cake worksheets. Notice how the results on the 'My profits' worksheet change too.

Think again

A summary worksheet combines values from several other worksheets. Why is it a good idea to include a summary worksheet?

In this lesson

You will learn:

→ how to work independently using your spreadsheet skills.

Add some useful features

In the last lesson you created a summary worksheet. In this lesson, you will use the skills you have learned in this unit to add some new features to the summary worksheet. The following features will make the spreadsheet more useful for your business.

● Show the number of sales for Pizza Napoli and Tiramisu Cake.

● Show the total profit per product – multiply the profit per portion by the number of portions sold.

● Show the total profit for your business – add together the profit for all your products.

Your finished summary worksheet will look similar to this one.

	A	B	C	
1	**My pizza snack bar profits**			
2				
3	**Product**	Pizza Napoli	Tiramisu Cake	
4				
5	Profit per portion	$ 0.61	$ 0.58	
6	Number of portions sold	30	25	
7				
8	Profit per product	$ 18.34	$ 14.58	
9				
10	**TOTAL PROFIT**	$ 32.92		
11				

You will find hints to help you in this lesson.

How to format the values

Create a row with the label 'Number of portions sold'. The values you enter in this row are your sales figures. Sales figures are the number of each product that you sell.

In the example shown above, the pizza snack bar has sold 30 portions of Pizza Napoli and 25 portions of Tiramisu Cake. But you can enter any numbers you like.

Don't worry if your numbers appear in currency format. It is easy to change the format. Use the 'Number Format' menu to select the 'General' format.

How to enter formulas

You need to enter two new formulas. These examples show the formulas you need.

Profit per product: To calculate the profit per product, multiply the profit per portion by the number of portions sold. The operator for multiply is *.

3	**Product**	Pizza Napoli
4		
5	Profit per portion	$ 0.61
6	Number of portions sold	30
7		
8	Profit per product	=B6*B5
9		

Total profit: To calculate the total profit, add together the profit from both the products on the worksheet.

8	Profit per product	$ 18.34	$ 14.58
9			
10	**TOTAL PROFIT**	=B8+C8	
11			

Activity

Create the 'My profits' worksheet shown in this lesson. Use the skills you have learned and the hints in this lesson.

Extra challenge

At the moment your pizza snack bar sells two products: Pizza Napoli and Tiramisu Cake. Add another recipe to the spreadsheet.

- Make a worksheet for your new recipe.
- Add the list of ingredients, the cost of the ingredients and the selling price of one portion.
- Calculate the profit per portion.
- Add the new product to the 'My profits' worksheet.

Explore more

Your spreadsheet shows the cost of making your products. The amount of money you need to make your products is called your budget. Talk to your family and friends to find out if they use a budget at home or at work.

Use your spreadsheet model

In this lesson

You will learn:

→ how to change the values in a spreadsheet

→ how to use a spreadsheet model to explore choices and make decisions.

Explore the effects of changes

The spreadsheet you have made uses formulas to calculate results. The spreadsheet is a mathematical model of your business. You can use the model to explore the effect of changes in the business.

How to use your spreadsheet model

If you change the values in your spreadsheet, the results of the calculations will change. In this example, a student has made changes to the Pizza Napoli worksheet.

The student then looks at the 'My profits' worksheet. The values have changed.

	A	B	C
1	My pizza snack bar		
2			
3	Recipe	Ingredients	
4	Pizza Napoli	500g flour	£ 0.75
5		2 cans tomato	$ 1.20
6		100g cheese	$ 1.00
7		10g oregano	$ 0.05
8		10g salt	$ 0.01
		5g yeast	$ 0.10
		TOTAL COST	$ 3.11
		Number of portions	8
		Cost per portion	$ 0.39
		Selling price	$ 1.50
17		PROFIT PER PORTION	$ 1.11
18			

> The student has changed the selling price of Pizza Napoli from $1.00 to $1.50.

> The profit per portion has automatically increased to $1.11.

	A	B	C
1	My pizza snack bar profits		
2			
3	Product	Pizza Napoli	Tiramisu Cake
4			
5	Profit per portion	$ 1.11	$ 0.58
6	Number of portions sold	30	25
7			
8	Profit per product	$ 33.34	$ 14.58
9			
10	TOTAL PROFIT	$ 47.92	
11			

> The total profits have increased to $47.92

Profits have increased. But the higher price could reduce the sales of Pizza Napoli. The student can use the spreadsheet model to explore the effect of this change. Here is an example.

	A	B	C
1	**My pizza snack bar profits**		
2			
3	**Product**	Pizza Napoli	Tiramisu Cake
4			
5	Profit per portion	$ 1.11	$ 0.58
6	Number of portions sold	22	25
7			
8	Profit per product	$ 24.45	$ 14.58
9			
10	**TOTAL PROFIT**	$ 39.03	

Activities

1 Change the values in your spreadsheet to explore the results of these changes:

- Increase the selling price of Pizza Napoli to $1.50 per portion.

- Decrease the number of portions sold of Pizza Napoli to 16.

- In the Tiramisu Cake recipe, decrease the cost of 1000 ml cream to $1.00.

- Increase the number of portions sold of Tiramisu Cake to 100.

2 Your business partners want to increase the profits for Pizza Napoli. They have asked you explore two options:

a Increase the number of portions from 8 to 12.

b Increase the selling price of one portion from $1.50 to $2.00.

Use your model to find out which option will make the most profit.

Extra challenge

Some cells in the spreadsheet store values that the user can change. An example is the 'Number of portions sold' value.

Use the 'Cell Styles' menus in the 'My profits' worksheet to highlight the values that the user can change.

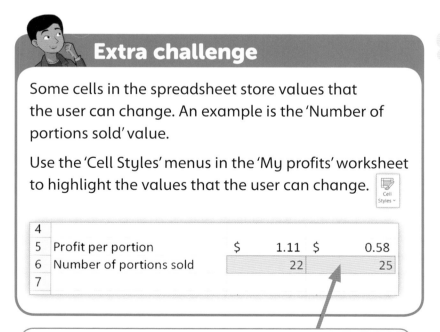

4			
5	Profit per portion	$ 1.11	$ 0.58
6	Number of portions sold	22	25
7			

These cells have been highlighted with a colour fill.

Think again

Many businesses decide on a 'mark-up' value to calculate their selling prices. In a snack bar, the mark-up might be 300%. This means that the selling price is three times the cost of the ingredients. Can you use your spreadsheet to calculate a 300% mark-up for the Tiramisu Cake?

Check what you know

You have learned

→ how to store text and number values using a spreadsheet

→ how to use spreadsheet formulas to calculate results

→ how to use a spreadsheet to help manage a business

→ how to explore the effect of changes to values.

Test

1 How do you change a value to a currency format?

2 What is the first thing you type when you create a formula?

3 When you are creating a formula, how do you insert a cell reference?

4 How can you change the width of a spreadsheet column?

5 Write what this cell reference means:

='My profits'!C8

6 How can you use a spreadsheet to explore the effect of making changes in your business?

 **Activities**

1 A group of students organised a cake sale to make money for charity. They made cakes to sell to students, teachers and parents.

The students used this spreadsheet to record the money they made.

	A	B	C
1	**School cake sale**		
2			
3	**Cake**	**Selling price**	**Number sold**
4	Cupcake	$ 0.50	36
5	Fruit cake	$ 3.50	6
6	Sponge cake	$ 4.50	9
7	Cherry cake	$ 3.00	7
8	Chocolate cake	$ 5.00	15

a Create the spreadsheet in your spreadsheet application.

b Add formulas to calculate the income from each type of cake.

c Add a formula to calculate the total income from all the cakes.

2 The students want to use their spreadsheet to calculate how much profit they have made for charity. They have added a separate worksheet to record their costs.

a Add this worksheet to your spreadsheet.

b Enter the labels and values.

c Enter a formula to calculate the total costs.

d On the 'Sales' worksheet, create a label for 'TOTAL PROFIT'.

e On the 'Sales' worksheet, enter a formula to calculate the total profit: subtract the total costs from the total income.

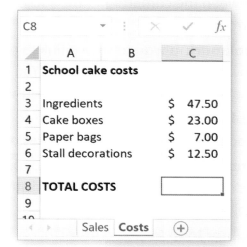

Self-evaluation

- I answered test questions 1 and 2.

- I started activity 1. I created a spreadsheet with labels and values. I added some formulas to the spreadsheet.

- I answered test questions 1–4.

- I completed activity 1.

- I answered all the test questions.

- I completed both activities.

Re-read any parts of the unit you feel unsure about. Try the test and activities again – can you do more this time?

Glossary

advantage a benefit or good point. Different ways of solving computer problems may have various advantages

algorithm a plan to solve a problem. It sets out the steps of the solution in the right order. A program plan is an example of an algorithm

'answer' block a block in Scratch that stores the most recent answer entered by the user in response to a question in a Scratch program

autofocus a feature of a digital camera that measures the distance between the camera and the subject. This allows the lens to focus correctly

bookmark a way to save a link to a web page that you like. The web browser saves your bookmarks. You can use the list of bookmarks to quickly find your favourite sites again

cable a long wire that is used to connect network devices together in a local area network (LAN). Cables may be copper or fibre optic

composition the arrangement of parts in an image such as a photo or drawing. The parts of a composition can include the foreground, the subject and the background

counter loop (or fixed loop) a loop that is controlled by a counter. You set the number of repeats at the top of the loop. When the loop reaches that number, the loop stops

conditional loop (or condition-controlled loop) a loop that is controlled by a logical test. The logical test is repeated with each repeat of the loop. In Scratch the loop stops when the logical test is True

coordinates two numbers that set the position of a point on a surface. The two numbers are called the x coordinate and the y coordinate

copyright the legal right of a person who has created text, images, music or any other content. Copyright prevents other people from using work without permission

costume sprites can change how they look. These different looks are called costumes in Scratch. Use a purple 'Looks' block to change a sprite's costume

crop to cut away part of an image when editing

degree a unit for measuring the size of an angle. A right angle is 90 degrees. To reverse the direction use a turn of 180 degrees

digital photo a photo made with a camera that records and stores images as digital data

disadvantage a problem or bad point. Different ways of solving computer problems may have various disadvantages

exit condition the method used to stop a loop. Different types of loop have different exit conditions

exposure the amount of light that is allowed to hit the camera's sensor

format the style of something or how it is organised. In a spreadsheet there are different number formats that you can use for values, such as 'Number', 'Currency', 'Percentage'

formula a set of instructions for a calculation. A spreadsheet formula calculates values using numbers, cell references and mathematical operators. Formulas are an important feature of spreadsheets. They allow you to make changes to the values so you can see how the changes affect the results of the calculations

frame the outer edges of an image

'go to' block a block with space for two numbers, an x coordinate and a y coordinate. You can enter any numbers into these two spaces. Then you can put the block into a program. It will make the sprite go to those coordinates

hub a type of switch

index a search engine index contains a summary of every page on the world wide web. The search engine uses the index to provide answers to web search questions

internet a wide area network (WAN) that connects computers across the world

ISO a setting on a digital camera that controls how sensitive the device is to light. High ISO settings make it possible to take photos with less light, but the quality of the images can be lower

key word a word you enter into a search engine. The search engine will find web pages that include the key word

left-aligned shown on the left of a page or cell

local area network (LAN) a network that connects computers in a single building or group of buildings

logical test a test that compares two values. The answer can be either True or False

login the details that a user enters to gain access to a network. A login is usually made up of a user name and a password

loop a program structure. Commands inside the loop will repeat

mathematical model a tool that uses formulas and equations to help a business find out what might happen in the future. You can use a spreadsheet to create a mathematical model. When you change values in the spreadsheet, you can see how the changes affect the business

meta tag a description of the content of a web page. A person reading a web page cannot see the meta tags, but search engines read and use meta tags

monochrome different tones of only one colour. A black and white photo is a monochromatic image

network a group of computers and other devices (such as printers) that are connected together so that they can share data and resources

network device hardware that is used to make a computer network operate, such as a server, a router or a hub

network software There are three different types of network software:

  1 software that is used to make a computer network operate

  2 application software that runs over a network, so all the users on the network can use it

  3 software that is used to manage a network

noise unwanted speckles and dots in digital images that were taken in darker conditions

password a code that a user enters to gain access to a network. Only the user knows their password

plagiarism copying another person's work and pretending it is your own work

profit the money that is left over after a business has made a product and sold it to a customer. You can calculate profit by subtracting costs from income

program plan the steps needed to solve a program. A programmer makes a plan before they start work. The program plan typically sets out the inputs, processes and outputs of the program

protocol a special rule that allows network devices to communicate with each other and share data

random unpredictable. For example, if a value is a random number you don't know what the number will be

repeat until loop a type of conditional loop. There is a test at the top of the loop. The commands inside the loop repeat until the logical test is True

retouch to remove mistakes or unwanted parts of an image. Retouching is sometimes called 'photoshopping', after a popular picture-editing application

right-aligned shown on the right of a page or cell

right-click to click using the right-hand mouse button. In most applications, right-clicking shows a menu that allows you to make changes to a selected area of text, values or an image

router a device that connects a local area network (LAN) to the internet

sample to record digital information. In photo editing, a clone tool samples pixels. These pixels can be copied to another part of the image when retouching

search engine software that searches for web pages. You enter key words or a question into a search box. The software finds web pages that match your key words

server a powerful computer used in a network. Each server in a network does a particular job. Examples are email server, print server and file server

server room a room where servers and other network devices are stored. A server room is securely locked and often has air conditioning to keep the servers cool

shutter speed the length of time the camera's shutter is open, allowing light to hit the sensor. Shutter speed is an important way of controlling exposure

smart device a household device that can connect to the internet. Connecting a device to the internet allows you to control remotely across the internet

spider a piece of software that a search engine uses in the web crawling process. Spiders visit web pages and collect information about each page. The information is used to create an index of the web

starting event an event that makes a program start to run. You use a yellow 'Events' block to set the starting event for a Scratch program

storyboard a way of planning a photo shoot using pictures to tell a story

subject the main object or person in a photo

switch a device used to connect network cables together. A switch decides which cable a message needs to be sent along to get to the right destination

variable a stored data value that can change as the program runs. A variable has a name. If you use the variable's name in your program, the computer will use the stored value

web crawling a method used by search engines to create an index of all the pages on the world wide web

web page a document that is made with HTML. The HTML comes to your computer through an internet connection. You see the web page in your web browser

website a collection of web pages. A website is owned by an organisation or individual. Websites usually contain web pages about a particular subject or topic

Wi-Fi another term for a wireless connection

wide area network (WAN) a network that connects computers and local area networks together across long distances

wired connection using a cable to connect a device to a local area network. Desktop computers are usually connected by a wired connection

wireless access point (WAP) a network device that allows wireless connection to a local area network (LAN)

wireless connection using a wireless access point (WAP) to connect a device to a local area network (LAN). Tablets and laptop computers are usually connected using a wireless connection

workflow the steps that need to be followed in order to complete a task

world wide web (www or web) the part of the internet that contains all the websites and web pages in the world. You use a web browser to view the web

x coordinate a number that tells you the left–right position of a point on a surface

y coordinate a number that tells you the up–down position of a point on a surface